WORSTED IN THE GAME

WORSTED IN THE GAME

Losers in Irish History

Edited by
CIARAN BRADY

'Our prayer is: "God save Ireland
    And pour blessings on her name."
May her sons be true when needed –
May they never feel as we did.
For, Shaun O'Dwyer *aglanna*,
    We're worsted in the game.'

(P. A. Sheehan, *Glenanaar*, 1905)

THE LILLIPUT PRESS

in association with Radio Telefís Éireann

1989

First published in 1989 by
THE LILLIPUT PRESS LTD
4 Rosemount Terrace, Arbour Hill,
Dublin 7, Ireland

Acknowledgments

These essays are based upon a companion series to the Thomas Davis
Lectures entitled 'The Losers', first broadcast on RTE Radio 1 between June
and September 1987. The publisher and editor would like to thank all
contributors for their co-operation, and in particular Michael Laffin who
suggested the title.

We are grateful for the encouragement and help given by Mr Michael
Littleton, General Editor of the Thomas Davis Lectures, and are happy to
acknowledge a grant in aid of publication from the Faculties of Arts
(Humanities) and Arts (Letters) of Trinity College, Dublin. Thanks also are
due to the National Library of Ireland, to the Library of Trinity College,
Dublin, and to Ms Pauline Codd for help with illustrations.

A CIP catalogue record for this title is available from The British Library.

ISBN 0 946640 35 1

Cover design by The Graphiconies
Typeset on a DTP Apple Macintosh Laser Printer
by Print-Forme, Santry, Dublin 9
Printed by The Guernsey Press Co. Ltd., Guernsey, Channel Islands

CONTENTS

INTRODUCTION: HISTORIANS AND LOSERS

CIARAN BRADY

THE CYNICAL OBSERVATION THAT historians side with the winners no longer carries conviction, in its original, most obvious sense at any rate. The time when history was written to recount the endeavours of great men gone for the education and edification of great men to be has long since passed; and for more than a century historical researchers have been engaged on a sustained campaign to uncover the lives of the poor, the oppressed and the inarticulate over long stretches of time. The results of such efforts, moreover, have been substantial. Over many decades social and economic historians have succeeded in reconstructing some of the most essential constituents of the lives of ordinary people, through the investigation of birth-rates and death-rates, family sizes, food supply, and movements in prices, wages and rents. Political historians have also played their part, in uncovering the records of parties and movements which were so often marginalized and repressed by the ruling powers of their own time. More recently the establishment of women's history as a recognized branch of study in its own right has been responsible for the discovery of a great deal of evidence concerning the lives of the largest and most persistently disadvantaged element in human history – and promises more to come. In all of these ways large groups of people discriminated against by history on economic, political and cultural grounds have been restored to their due place in the record, and historians have liberated themselves from their enslavement to one whom William James described as 'that bitch-goddess, success'.

There is, however, a rather more subtle way in which historians still cling to her skirts. Deep-rooted within the historical imagination is a conviction that certain events (or individuals who shaped them) have established a claim to pre-eminence that seems to be both self-evident and self-justifying.

The assumption is in many cases perfectly valid – who would doubt the significance of the French Revolution or of V. I. Lenin? Yet the uncritical manner in which it has so often been applied has led to serious distortion and to error in many other cases. At its most extreme, the untested assertion that some events have been invested with a special role within the larger historical process can be seen in the great system theories of history which posit a fundamental pre-determining force; the ever-intervening providential hand, the survival imperative, or the human mind's journey toward self-realization. Marxist historians, it is worth noting, have in general been wary of crude determinism of this kind, and few professionals, whatever their ideological viewpoint, have been prepared to commit themselves to such imprisoning views of their discipline.

Yet in less obvious ways the sense that certain past events were linked together in some necessary larger pattern continues to permeate historical thought. Its influence over certain – now rather old-fashioned – Marxist schools of history is well known, but it may also be seen in the work of historians who would disavow any overt political affiliations. It appears, for instance, in the assumption common to American historians that because slavery was fundamentally incompatible with American culture, war between the north and the south was at some point inevitable. It is manifest in broader canvas in that British historiographical tradition once analyzed by Herbert Butterfield as 'the Whig interpretation' which has traced the central thread of England's history through those events and individuals credited with the extension of Englishmen's liberty and of the country's material progress.

The Whig view of history has never been overly sympathetic to the case of England's island neighbour. But the Irish, as we have now become more aware, had nevertheless developed a whiggish perspective of their own, in which the country's progress toward national self-determination and the survival and consolidation of its people's commitment to the religious culture of Catholicism were assumed to be the organizing themes of their history, determining the character of interpretation and fixing the agenda for further research. This hallowed tradition has come under critical scrutiny, as has its English counterpart. Recent research on all aspects of Irish history has produced much valuable new evidence, subverting some long-cherished views and seriously redefining others. There may be, as some observers have noted, a tendency for sustained critiques of this kind to harden into orthodoxies no less rigid than those they opposed, but as yet there is little evidence of such a development in modern Irish historiography. It appears to a degree in some recent overviews of Irish history and in more overtly political essays by authors with an historical training; it may be found also in the unspoken assumption of some researchers that every item within the traditional historical account is by definition subject to reversal. Yet the common belief that there is a school of historical revisionists bent upon replacing old nationalist orthodoxies with an alternative framework oversimplifies the subtlety and complexity as well as the sheer disputatiousness of current historical writing.

There is, however, a residual sense in which Irish historians in common with their colleagues everywhere have been mislead by success. From the beginning of their training historians have been conditioned to study and to write only about *what actually happened*. Such an austere refusal to speculate about might-have-beens and non-events has doubtless been most salutary in its distancing of history from the lists of political controversy. But fidelity to Ranke's famous credo, *Wie es eigentlich gewesen ist*, has rendered historians over-cautious in their approach to those possibilities which almost became realities, and to those individuals who nearly brought them about. There are, then, groups of historical actors who are losers in a quite specific sense: not the weak and downtrodden who rarely had a chance to partake in the historical processes which affected them, but rather figures who for a long time or for a brief moment possessed the knowledge or the power to act decisively in the midst of historical change, who used that capacity and who failed. These are the losers under consideration here: players equipped with their counters and with a clear knowledge of the rules, who chanced their fortune and were worsted in the game. Every country has had its share of such figures and Ireland, by the manner in which its history has been shaped, has had more than most. Their rehabilitation is a service long since due to them; but more importantly it is an essential pre-condition to the re-discovery of our true past.

Winning connotes one clear result; losing implies several.

None of the figures presented here lost in precisely the same way or in the same degree, or over comparable issues. Yet they have received similar treatment at the hands of posterity. Several have suffered loss through persistent misinterpretation of their aims and their actions by generations of commentators, favourable and unfavourable. For example, the unfortunate Diarmait MacMorrough retains his reputation as an irresponsible adventurer, ready to barter with the sovereignty of his native land; Edward Carson is lauded by some and reviled by others for a settlement in Ulster which left him bitterly disappointed. Others have been the victims of subtler ironies: Tyrconnell was not the leader of an independent Catholic Ireland as he has sometimes been portrayed; the Home Rule party thrived upon tactics and objectives in a way its founder Isaac Butt could never have contemplated. Many more have simply been forgotten. John de Courcy is a shadowy figure of whom little direct evidence has survived. Thomas Butler, earl of Ormond, and Archbishop King have left rich archives but remain without a serious modern biography. Few read Fintan Lalor.

In these cases history has sanctioned the rights of the winners to consign their rivals to obscurity. But in some instances history's role in such rites of immolation has been rather more positive. The opening and closing chapters of this book deal in different ways with cases of this kind. Conor mac Nesa has been made known to us only through his historians' concern to present a fictionalized portrait designed to harness what power the historical man retained in folk-memory to the purposes of the Christian mission. What remains to be known about the original Ulster king is not then some genuine relique, but a wholly artificial construct. Mac Nesa's fate has been shared, though in different circumstances, by James Connolly. The depth of Connolly's concern with class politics, his commitment to revolution and his mistrust of nationalist agitation all proved to be intensely embarrassing to politicians and historians after 1916, quickening their efforts to enshroud Connolly within the penumbra of the heroic nationalist canon and to obscure the highly subversive analysis of Irish history and society that led him at length to join in the rebellion.

As Paul Bew points out, however, Connolly had contributed in some measure to posterity's judgment of him. In the spring of 1916 the leader of the Irish Citizen Army gravely overestimated the appeal of his movement to the Irish working class and to the poor, and underestimated nationalism's capacity to rekindle deeper imperatives of resentment and self-affirmation. In this he resembles some of history's other losers who similarly misjudged the nature and the power of the political and ideological forces with which they were engaged. Henry Flood has suffered his share from unfair comparison with his more flamboyant and less consistent rival, Grattan. But the eclipse of his reputation, as David Dickson argues, was due in no small degree to his uncritical faith in the workings of the parliamentary system within which he had matured and to his consequent misperception of the issues which he faced in the 1770s and 1780s. The same high confidence in the virtues of the parliamentary process under which he himself had prospered blighted the later career of John Redmond, the once uncompromising Parnellite who remained convinced, in the face of mounting evidence to the contrary, that the resolution of Ireland's ills was to be found in the debating chambers and committee rooms of Westminister. Irish history's most notorious case of political misjudgment is, of course, represented by Diarmait MacMurrough. Reviled for centuries as the first in a long line of Ireland's traitors, Mac Murrough, by inviting Strongbow and his friends to come to his aid, had simply employed a rather conventional tactic in a regional dynastic contest. That the Anglo-French adventurers were influenced by Angevin dynastic politics and local concerns in Wales and the West Country to take a far more ambitious view of their presence in Ireland was a matter which he could hardly have been expected to anticipate.

Because they were so overt, and because, in the latter two cases, their consequences were so momentous, failures of this kind have been registered often enough by history: even though, with the certainty of hindsight, they have been treated usually with harshness, insensitivity and disregard. Yet there is a parallel set of more subtle miscalculations which has occasioned even greater neglect. This applies to those individuals whose experience of defeat was due neither to ignorance nor misperception of the forces of change operative in their time, but rather to an acute awareness of such forces and a determination to resist or reshape them. One such instance is represented by William Bedell, the seventeenth-century Church of Ireland bishop whose concern with the sharpening of religious divisions in his time confirmed his own commitment to the spread of religious reform through education rather than coercion in a manner long since abandoned. It was a similar perception of the long-term perils entailed by the course embarked upon by his fellow Protestants that impelled another ecclesiastic, Archbishop King, to advance his own vision of the Ireland toward which his contemporaries should aspire, which for all its weaknesses and inconsistencies was, as Patrick Kelly suggests, based upon a far clearer sense of the dilemma confronting the eighteenth-century colonial elite than most of their number were willing to allow. An unheeded prophet of a rather different type was James Fintan Lalor. Lalor's vision of Ireland was, as Mary Daly argues, romantic and reactionary; but it too was fuelled by a deep foreboding of the imminent break-up of the traditional rural community and of the emergence of economic rivalries and inequalities among Ireland's tenant farmers which were to become manifest in the decades following his death.

The alternative Irelands held out by these men, even when sympathetically viewed, will not now command much respect. For they were themselves replete with ambiguities and contradictions which would have rendered them quite unreal in the form in which they were first presented. Yet such losers remain of central importance to the course of Irish history precisely because they embodied and gave voice to the most profound tensions of their times in a manner in which their less sensitive contemporaries, and subsequent commentators, blinded by what came after, could not match. It is in this sense that Isaac Butt may be counted among the most interesting of this type. Butt who moved from the Orangeism of his youth to lay the foundations of the Home Rule agitation in which he was soon eclipsed by harder and more angry men, is often viewed as a minor and somewhat pathetic figure in the Irish historical canon. Yet there is, as W. J. Mc Cormack's suggestive essay argues, a deeper unity to Butt's literary and political career in his quest to discover by means of public action a resolution of the inner dilemmas (sensed also by Bedell and King) arising from the Irish Protestant's uneasy relations with his English governors and with his fellow-countrymen.

Such men, however noble their ideals, were in the strictest sense reactionaries, resisting historical movements which were already in the ascendant. It may be said then that they consciously risked and to a degree hastened their relegation to the ash-heap of history. But other men's fate was to be rather more tragic. For there remains one further group of Ireland's losers whose ultimate defeat arose not from some heroic last stand against the future, but from their desire to accelerate and to dominate the forces of change and to their all-too-great success in doing so. One such figure was John de Courcy, the medieval adventurer, whose attempt to establish an autonomous lordship in Ulster came so close to success that Gaelic chieftains and English kings alike determined that no similar enterprise would again be essayed once the force of de Courcy's character began to wane. More complex was the case of Thomas Butler, earl of Ormond. That great magnate's success in exploiting the Tudor concern to establish a united kingdom in Ireland for his own dynastic interests was initially so complete that he at length persuaded both Englishmen and Irishmen to abandon the project altogether. In the same way the ruthless manner in which Richard Butler, earl of Tyrconnell, exercised the power of the Irish executive to advance the Catholic interest ensured that that interest would be suppressed with even greater ruthlessness by an Irish legislature determined to assert its claims against both royal government and the majority of the island's people. In our own century, losing of this sort was to be the experience of Edward Carson. An immensely gifted advocate whose tireless efforts convinced the British government that Home Rule would be unworkable, Carson's case was so persuasive that the same government itself finally concluded that only partition and the break-up of his beloved Union could solve Britain's problems in Ireland.

The losers presented here, either among the most progressive or the most reactionary, the most tragic or most pathetic, do not make up a comprehensive group. Other equally likely candidates from every century might have been considered for inclusion; doubtless many more have been neglected simply because the importance of their case continues to be under-rated. Yet the individuals selected share an importantly representative character. It is not merely because of the extent of their failure or of its intrinsic pathos that they command attention; nor merely because of the gravity of the events which their failure set in train. These men are significant because they demonstrate in their different ways the complexity of the process by which historical change is effected. They offer proof that history moves not through slowly unfolding, unilinear patterns, nor through cyclical revolutions, but through contingencies of force and circumstance, whose conjuncture could not have been predicted and could never be repeated. The recovery of Ireland's losers, then, is not simply an interesting diversion, but a means of undermining that impulse toward uncritical pattern-making to which historical writing is so susceptible. The losers make clear that Ireland's past is neither the record of one dominant theme nor even a set of counter-themes. Instead it is a series of turning-points offering alternative options, any one of which, if chosen, would have reshaped the course of Irish history in ways which are wholly different from each other.

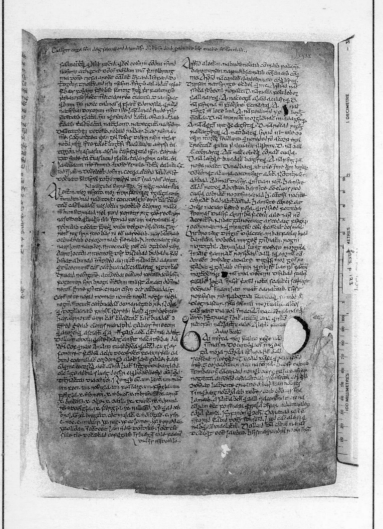

Tale of the death of Conor mac Nesa from The Book of Leinster
(twelfth-century MS, Library of Trinity College, Dublin)

I

CONCHOBAR mac NESA (? first century AD) and the Triumph of Christianity

LIAM BREATNACH

CONCHOBAR MAC NESA BELONGS to a period for which we have no contemporary written records. This essay, then, largely concerns the historical value of those later sources which purport to give an account of his career. They date from a time when Ireland was not only itself Christianized but was also playing an important missionary role in Britain and Western Europe, and we can hardly expect an accurate and unbiassed account of the pagan past from these sources. Conchobar has been chosen as a representative of pagan Ireland. Any of the other pre-Christian figures, Cormac mac Airt for example, would have served equally well, but insofar as mac Nesa symbolizes a pagan Ireland which ultimately yielded to Christianity, he can be regarded as among the earliest of Irish history's losers.

In the early sources Conchobar mac Nesa appears as the king of the *Ulaid*, 'the Ulstermen', with his seat at Emain Macha, now Navan Fort near Armagh, and is pictured as living at the beginning of the Christian era. He, alongside Cú Chulainn, is a central character in the large body of tales known as the *Rúraíocht* or the Ulster Cycle, centred around the doings of the Ulstermen in remote historical times.

In constructing mac Nesa's 'biography' from the various sources which deal with him, one could take first the tale *Compert Chonchobair*, 'The Birth of Conchobar', which gives an account of his birth in unusual circumstances to Ness, daughter of Eochaid Sálbuide, king of Ulster. Then one could pick out the high points of his career as king of Ulster, which is said to have lasted for fifty years. Of these the most important would of course have been the conflict of the Ulstermen with the other provinces of Ireland, related in *Táin Bó Cúailnge*. Finally, one could round off one's 'biography' with the tale *Aided Chonchobair*, 'The Death of Conchobar'. This account of his death can be summarized briefly. During the course of a battle between the Ulstermen and the Connaughtmen, Cet the Connacht warrior had shot from a sling the brain of Mes Gegra into Conchobar's head. Fíngen, Conchobar's physician, judged that Mes Gegra's brain should remain lodged in Conchobar's head and that any excitement or strain would dislodge it, causing Conchobar's death. So things remained until Conchobar heard news of the crucifixion of Christ, in whom he is said to have believed, and his distress at his inability to fight to defend Christ caused Mes Gegra's brain to spring from his head, resulting in his death.

What are we to make of these accounts? First, they were written so long after the events they claim to describe that we cannot be sure that they deal with real historical persons and events at all. Certain scholars hold that at least some of the tales of the Ulster Cycle dimly reflect an earlier real historical state of affairs. Others stress the mythological aspects of these tales and regard them as having undergone the process of euhemerization, whereby the characters of the tales were made into historical personages. Secondly, as is clear from the reference to Christ's crucifixion, we are not dealing with purely pagan accounts. Thirdly, apart from a few references to Ireland in classical sources, the only direct evidence we have for pre-Christian Ireland is archaeological. Archaeological remains do tell us about the type of dwellings people lived in, the kind of agriculture they practised, their household goods, weapons, etc., but they do not name individuals or give any of the narrative history which written sources provide; so we have nothing with which we can directly compare these later accounts to check their veracity. One of the most instructive approaches, therefore, is to examine the environment in which they were produced and see how they reflect it rather than the time in which they are set.

Our knowledge of early Ireland comes down to us in two languages. Some written sources are in Latin, dating from the coming of Christianity in the fifth century onwards, but the majority are in Irish. The earliest surviving Irish text is generally taken to be the *Amra Coluim Chille*, a lament for Colum Cille, written shortly after the saint's death in 597, but it is only from the seventh century onwards that we find a substantial body of written material in Irish. The form of the language in which our earliest texts are written is known as Old Irish.

The sources written in Latin are almost entirely ecclesiastical in nature. Ecclesiastical texts, such as saints' lives, calendars, hymns, devotional texts, etc., have also come down to us in Old Irish, but besides these we find in the vernacular a large body of secular material, such as genealogies, histories, annals, sagas, praise-poetry, satire and law-texts. Our sources are not confined to contemporary matters but also concern Ireland's prehistory, and various criteria, especially linguistic, show these to be no later than the seventh century.

The earliest, seventh-century account of Conchobar mac Nesa, *Aided Chonchobair*, 'The Death of Conchobar', was written when Ireland had been steadily Christianized from the time of Patrick two hundred years previously. By the seventh century the Church had achieved an important position and monasteries were centres of wealth, learning and influence. The upper echelons of society, kings and nobility, and also the secular learned classes, had become Christian, and scholars have long recognized that the early sagas, poetry, genealogies, histories, etc., emanated from such an environment. Recent research has shown that the Brehon laws, thought by some to derive from law-schools little influenced by Christianity, in fact also had a large ecclesiastical input in their drafting and promulgation.

In the context of the law the supreme position was of course held by the law of Scripture, as the law dictated by God. There also existed the traditional native Irish law and the theorizing of early Irish jurists concerning the foundations of law reveal how the Church adapted itself to early Irish society. One of the more widely disseminated products of such theorizing appears (typically) in the form of a narrative telling how Patrick, after meeting and converting Lóegaire, the king of Tara, dealt with the question of Irish law and customs: Dubthach moccu Lugair, a *fili* 'poet', recited for Patrick all the laws of the Irish, and Patrick expunged all that conflicted 'with the word of God and the Christian conscience'. The rest was allowed to remain as complementary to the law of Scripture, because, as the Old Irish text puts it, *Ataat mára i recht aicnid ro-siachtatar nád roacht recht litre*, 'There are many things covered in the law of Nature which the law of Scripture did not reach.'

The 'law of Nature' was used in reference to native Irish law, and was a very important concept in the efforts of the early Irish learned classes to reconcile Christian teaching with traditional native practices. The term can be used in the sense that St Paul used it in his well-known passage on the natural law and the Gentiles (Rom. 2:14): 'Indeed, when Gentiles, who do not have the law, do by nature things required by the law, they are a law for themselves, even though they do not have the law.' The usual distinction made, then, is three-fold: the law of the Old Testament, of the New Testament, and of Nature, which is further identified with native Irish law. These distinctions, which themselves all have some basis in Scripture, provide a framework within which the early Irish Christian learned classes could justify those native practices which clearly did not derive from Scripture.

This model had been devised as early as the seventh century, and was not only applied to the contemporary situation, but accommodated the earlier history of Ireland or, more accurately, was the means by which prevailing views could be projected onto the pagan past. Thus sages of the remote past such as Amairgen, Morand, etc., gave just judgments because they had the 'justice of natural law', this being due to the inspiration of the Holy Ghost. They are depicted as living a righteous life, lacking only the knowledge of the Christian faith. Other accounts go even further, with pre-Christian poets foretelling the Incarnation of Christ, as well as the coming of Christianity to Ireland.

This process of backward projection applied not only to the learned classes, but also to kings. Cormac mac Airt, for instance, was said to have believed in God long before the coming of Patrick, and therefore to have refused to be buried alongside his pagan predecessors in *Brug na Bóinne* (modern Newgrange). In the same way, as mentioned earlier, Conchobar mac Nesa is said to have known of the crucifixion and to have died a believer.

These constructs, while of no value for the history of pre-Christian Ireland, are useful in determining how the Christian Church saw itself relating to the secular powers in the seventh and later centuries. They reflect not only a self-confident Church which has converted the major dynasties and which has great influence in secular affairs, but also a Church that was prepared to accept native customs and traditions as long as these were not seen to contradict the teachings of Christianity. Coupled with this acceptance would have been a desire to provide a historical justification for them. Hence the ascribing of divine inspiration to the mythical pre-Christian sages, who were believed to have laid the foundations of native Irish laws and institutions. Their authority would then have been comparable to that of the Old Testament prophets.

This tolerant attitude of the ecclesiastics resulted in the creation and transmission of the extremely rich and varied vernacular literature of Old Irish, and many of the pre-Christian *elements* in this literature enable us to reconstruct a partial picture of pagan Ireland.

It is quite likely that certain more unpalatable pagan practices survived marginally among the lower echelons of society. Take, for instance, the frequent references to druids in early sources. In the contemporary context of the seventh and later centuries they appear as little more than wizards rather than as the priests of an official, publicly supported religion. Frequent condemnations of various sorcerous practices shows that these too existed in early Ireland, and indeed many continued as pishogues down to our own time.

The important fact, however, is that we have no writings which come from a pagan learned class. The literate learned classes of early Ireland can be broadly divided into two: ecclesiastics, and a secular literate class known as *filid*, usually translated as 'poets', although this translation is not entirely satisfactory. The distinction between the two is not always strictly maintained, and we quite often find ecclesiastics functioning as poets or poets entering the Church. Early texts on the poets make it quite clear that they were expected to live according to a strictly Christian standard of behaviour. For example, the eighth-century text *Uraicecht na Ríar* states the *fili* must have 'purity of learning, and purity of mouth, and purity of hand and marital union and purity consisting of being innocent of theft and plunder and illegality, and purity of body, that he have only one wife, for one perishes through illicit cohabitation aside from one chaste woman on lawful nights'. Furthermore, in texts purporting to give an account of the coming of Christianity to Ireland, such as the *Life of Patrick*, the poets are depicted as being favourable to the new religion.

The very introduction of writing into Ireland indeed, was a by-product of Christianity, a 'religion of the book' which required that its priesthood be literate in the language of its sacred texts, and thus the creation of a secular learned class, literate in the vernacular, could only have proceeded under the aegis of the Church. Unlike Rome, where literacy long antedates the rise of Christianity, we do not have in early Ireland a class of literate pagans, and so all our sources for the defeat of paganism and the spread of Christianity in early Ireland come from one side only, that of the victors. On the other hand a vigorous oral tradition predated Christianity in Ireland and continued for a long time afterwards. We must assume this, among other reasons, to account for the many parallels between Irish tradition and that of other Celtic-speaking peoples, especially the Welsh, and also to explain elements of pagan origin in early Irish literature.

This debt to oral tradition is clearly recognized in early Irish sources. At the beginning of the great eighth-century collection of Irish law known as the *Senchas Már*, the question is asked as to what has preserved Irish law, and the answer begins: *Comchuimne da sen, tindnacul cluaise di araile, díchetal filed*, 'The joint memory of the ancients, transmission from ear to ear, the chanting of poets', although then going on to speak of it 'being augmented by the law of Scripture' (*tórmach ó recht litre*). The continuation of oral tradition into early Christian times is also attested to in our sources. In these the *filid* are distinguished from a lower order of poets called bards. The *filid* are depicted as literate and learned, having undergone a rigorous academic training, whereas the bards, whose ability in versification is a natural talent, have at best some degree of literacy, while others are clearly illiterate. This distinction between *filid* and bards can hardly be much earlier than the seventh century, from which can be dated the rise of a secular literate class and the development from literacy in Latin to significant literacy in Irish.

Doubtless, among the unlettered, pagan traditions were transmitted at the oral level, but to what extent we cannot be certain as we have no recordings of the oral traditions of the period. What we know of non-literate societies would indicate that much was altered with the passing of time, and that the oral traditions of the seventh century, say, would have been quite different from those of the second or third. What we can be certain of is that those who had access to writing were Christianized, and that they screened out the more unpalatable aspects of paganism. As one law text (*Cáin Fhuithirbe*) dating from *c.* 680 AD asserts, *ro dílsiged la dub in díchubus*, 'that which is contrary to [the Christian] conscience has been made forfeit by ink', or in other words the very act of writing entails a censorship of pagan beliefs.

Any account of pagan Ireland and the eventual triumph of Christianity, has to be very cautious in its use of the early Irish sources, and much will be little more than informed speculation. The partial picture of pagan Ireland that we can build up from later literary survivals may be complemented by evidence from the literature of other Celtic-speaking peoples. Reasons for the success of Christianity can be ascribed to various factors such as the enormous prestige of the Roman Empire, of which Christianity had been the official religion since the early fourth century.

Although the Irish had never been made part of the Roman Empire they had been in close contact with it – mostly, admittedly, as raiders – from an early period. The personal example of individual Christians, including traders and missionaries, provided another impetus. Patrick himself was captured during an Irish raid on Roman Britain and spent many years in Ireland as a slave. Doubtless there were many before him who would have formed the nucleus of a Christian community in Ireland. Thirdly, until the coming of the Vikings, Ireland, unlike Gaul or Britain, was not subject to the invasions of new groups of pagans from outside. Thus, once Christianity was established in Ireland, the only thing that could have thwarted it would have been a deliberate policy of persecution. As far as we can tell there were no Christian martyrs in Ireland.

Christianity was not simply a new set of beliefs but brought with it many of the attributes of the culturally more prestigious Roman Empire, such as literacy.

The process of Christianization did not of course result in a romanized Ireland. This process was inevitably a gradual one, especially when we remember that it was not imposed by force. The Church accommodated native institutions and practices, so that the Ireland reflected in our earliest sources appears a complex mixture of Christian and native elements, with the Church as the dominant and guiding intellectual force. Pagan Ireland survives only in a very attenuated form.

As no written narrative dates from the pre-Christian period, we cannot, therefore, speak of a biography of Conchobar mac Nesa, or of any other figure of the pagan past. Our early Irish sources are a classic example of the axiom that history is written by the victors.

FURTHER READING

Two recent works on the nature of literacy (and the differences between societies with and without writing) are by Jack Goody; *The Logic of Writing and the Organization of Society* (Cambridge 1986) and *The Interface between the Written and the Oral* (Cambridge 1987)

For the learned classes in early Ireland see Liam Breatnach, *Uraicecht na Ríar: The Poetic Grades in Early Irish Law* (Dublin 1987).

For other topics touched upon in this essay see Tomás Ó Cathasaigh, 'Pagan survivals: the evidence of early Irish narrative', *Irland and Europa: die Kirche im Frühmittelalter*, eds P. Ní Chatháin and M Richer (Stuttgart 1984), pp. 291-307; Donnchadh Ó Corráin, 'Historical Need and Literary Narrative', *Proceedings of the Seventh International Congress of Celtic Studies* (Oxford 1986), pp. 141-58; N. B. Aitchison, 'The Ulster Cycle: heroic image and historical reality', *Journal of Medieval History*, 13 (1987), pp. 87-116; Donnchadh Ó Corráin, Liam Breatnach, Aidan Breen, 'The Laws of the Irish', *Peritia*, 3 (1984), pp. 382-438; Donnchadh Ó Corráin, 'Irish vernacular law and the Old Testament', *Irland und die Christenheit: Bibelstudien und Mission*, eds P. Ní Chatháin and M. Richter (Stuttgart 1987), pp. 284-307.

II

DIARMAIT MacMURROUGH* (1110 - 71)
and the Coming of the Anglo-French

DONNCHADH Ó CORRÁIN

DIARMAIT MACMURROUGH, KING OF Leinster, died in 1171. His death-notice in the *Annals of Tigernach* reads:

Diarmait MacMurrough, king of Leinster and the Ostmen, the man who troubled Banba and destroyed Ireland, after mustering the foreigners and after ruining the Irish, after plundering and razing churches and territories, died at the end of a year of an insufferable disease, through the miracles of Finnian, Columcille and other saints whose churches he plundered.

The seventeenth-century *Annals of the Four Masters*, put together at a time of heightened national consciousness, have an even more colourful entry, based, as is evident, on *Tigernach:*

Diarmait MacMurrough, king of Leinster, by whom Ireland was made a trembling sod – after having brought over the Saxons, after having done extensive injuries to the Irish, after plundering and burning many churches, as Kells, Clonard etc. – died before the end of a year of an insufferable and unknown disease for he became putrid while still alive, through the miracles of God, Colmcille and Finnian and the other saints of Ireland whose churches he profaned and burned some time before; and he died at Ferns without making a will, without penance, without the body of Christ, without unction, as his evil deeds deserved.

There are biblical resonances – even reminiscences – about this account. According to the *Acts of the Apostles* (12:20), when king Herod attacked the nascent Church he was struck down by an

*For the sake of clarity the spelling 'Dermot', 'Dermott' and 'Diarmaid' in the cited texts have been consistently rendered as 'Diarmait'.

angel of the Lord, was eaten up with worms, and died. Even more, it is an echo of the story of Antiochus as told in 2 *Machabees* 9: when Anthiochus IV, king of Syria, and oppressor of the Jews, attempted to ravage Jerusalem, God struck him down with a terrible disease, he grew unbearably foul whilst living, was eaten by worms, and so died. The wicked king is struck down by the judgment of God – and clearly in the eyes of some clerical writers MacMurrough was an example of this judgment and a king comparable in his wickedness to Antiochus IV. We will see, however, that not all twelfth-century writers shared this opinion.

Giraldus Cambrensis in his *Expugnatio Hibernica* gives a sketch of MacMurrough:

Diarmait was tall and well-built, a brave and warlike man amongst his people, whose voice was hoarse as a result of having been in the din of battle. He preferred to be feared by all rather than loved. He treated his nobles harshly and brought to prominence men of humble rank. He was inimical towards his own people and hated by others. 'All men's hands were against him and he was hostile to all men.'

Giraldus tells how he ravished Dervorgilla. All subsequent writers have relied heavily – and perhaps unhistorically – on this. It is, after all, a good tale. In addition, he puts into the mouth of Rory O'Connor, king of Ireland, a speech in which he makes remarks about MacMurrough which are close to ones the O'Connor interest may well have had:

See how the enemy of his country, that despot over his own people and universal enemy, previously driven from his country, has now returned flanked by the arms of foreigners, to bring about our common ruin. For begrudging his own people their prosperity, he has introduced into the country men of foreign race to the end that, supported by the ferocity of this hateful people, he may more successfully exert against us that malice which he could not effectively exert unaided. So this man, himself our enemy, has brought in a race most hostile to ours which has long been eager to rule us all alike, Diarmait included ... he had not even spared himself in order that no one at all may be spared ... This is the man who formerly persecuted his subjects with an unrestrained tyranny. This is the man who is now taking this barbarous action against all of us with the aid of foreign forces.

This is stirring rhetoric – and is very much meant to be, but it is likely that it does reflect views with which Giraldus came into contact during his visits to Ireland in 1183 and 1185-6.

The story of MacMurrough's treachery – for it was seen as just that by many writers – has lost little in the telling down to our own day. MacMurrough became known in Irish as *Diarmait na nGall*, 'Diarmait of the foreigners', certainly in the fifteenth and sixteenth centuries, and probably earlier. Hugh MacCurtain, a traditional Gaelic historian, writing however in English, in 1717 states:

Diarmait MacMurrough, king of Leinster, committed the barbarous Rape upon Dearbhorgall, prince of Breifne's wife. This prince, Tighearnan O Ruairc, was a virtuous holy man, and warlike withal; he immediately complained of the wrong done him to king Roderick; who began to espouse the cause of O Ruairc, marched into Leinster, with a strong party of armed men, at last engag'd in battle with Diarmait, and gave him a signal overthrow ... he fled over to Bristol in England, and understanding there, that king Henry II of England was then in Aquitaine, he hasten'd over to him, and with all submission offered to subject himself and his kingdom of Leinster to the crown of England, if by his assistance he could recover it and procure peace from Roderick O'Connor, king of Ireland.

Various versions of this, with various embellishments, have been the staple of the school-books. Some accounts stress the immorality of MacMurrough's behaviour in running off with the wife of the king of Breifne, and they have good authority for it in the *Annals of Clonmacnoise s.a.* 1152:

Diarmait MacMurrough, king of Leinster, took the lady Dervorgill, daughter of Morrogh O'Melaghlin and wife of Teyrnan O'Royrck, with her cattle with him, and he kept her for a long space to satisfie his insatiable, carnal and adulterous lust. She was procured and induced thereunto by her unadvised brother, Melaghlin, for some abuses of her husband Teyrnan done before.

This, we can be sure, is the view of the seventeenth-century translator/editor of these annals – and the charge of sexual immorality – repeated in more or less flamboyant terms – combined with that of being a traitor surely damned him. Given the historiography and the smug moral climate of Ireland in the early and mid-twentieth century, it is not surprising that there was no national commemoration in 1969 of the 800th anniversary of the most important event with which MacMurrough was connected, the Anglo-French invasion in 1169. And when a stone tablet was put up at Baginbun that year, commemorating the landing of the Anglo-French, it was broken in a few days. In a sense, Diarmait MacMurrough is one of the centre-points of our uncomfortable, ambiguous relationship with our past – and dare I say? – with our present. And the discomfort is not confined to the school texts: it is very much present amongst the historians. Diarmait MacMurrough belonged to the Uí Chennselaig dynasty, which ruled south Leinster from early Christian times and which produced the kings of the province from the reign of Diarmait's great-grandfather, the powerful Diarmait mac Máel na mBó, king of Leinster and of the Ostmen, who ruled from 1042 to 1072. MacMurrough, then, was no Johnny-come-lately: he belonged to one of the greatest dynastic families in Ireland. He was born in 1110 or 1111. We know little or nothing about his early life, though it had been generally believed that he was educated by Aed Mac Crimthainn, abbot of Terryglass, one of the scribes of the *Book of Leinster*. This hare was started by a mistake made by Eugene O'Curry in 1861.

For Rev. Professor G. T. Stokes, writing in 1892, Aed Mac Crimthainn and the *Book of Leinster* did not do MacMurrough much good as a student:

The *Book of Leinster* written ... by the tutor to whom MacMurrough's education was entrusted ... Any of you can now consult in our various libraries and there you will find a volume which lay in the library and exercised the attention of Diarmait's early days ... The *Book of Leinster* is most valuable ... in setting forth the social life, the habits, customs, poetry and literary influences amid which Diarmait MacMurrough and men like him were cradled and reared ... MacMurrough's character may be tested by a modern rule. Examine a man's library and you may fairly gauge his habits and character. Examine the *Book of Leinster* and you will not be surprised that Diarmait MacMurrough's career was stained by bloodshed, vice and falsehood.

Of course, MacMurrough was not educated at Terryglass, his supposed teacher was his own contemporary, and there is not a shred of evidence to show that MacMurrough ever saw the *Book of Leinster*, much less read it. He was fostered out amongst the aristocracy, the Uí Cháellaide, a family whose lordship lay to the west of his own homeland of Uí Chennselaig. When king he treated members of that family very generously and promoted some of them politically and in the Church. However, MacMurrough's youth and early manhood are otherwise obscure.

His elder brother, Énna, ruled Leinster from 1117 to his death in 1126. Then the king of Ireland, Turlough O'Connor, invaded Leinster, deposed the 'son of Mac Murchada' and appointed his own son Conor king of Leinster. This did not go down well and in 1127 the Leinstermen joined forces with the Ostmen of Dublin and revolted against the rule of O'Connor. Curtis and other writers before him thought that this revolt was led by the sixteen year-old MacMurrough: 'inspired by a vigorous young prince, Dermot MacMurrough' – but this is doubtful. In fact MacMurrough first appears in the annals as king of Leinster in 1132, in which year he perpetrated a notorious outrage on the abbess of Kildare. The appointment of this the most prestigious ecclesiastical office-holder in Leinster was usually in the gift of the king of Leinster, and MacMurrough simply wanted his own appointee when the office was held by a north-Leinster abbess. He proceeded to disqualify her. As the *Annals of Loch Cé* have it:

The house of the abbess of Kildare was seized by the Uí Chennselaig against the successor of St Brigit and was burned together with a large portion of the church and a large number of people were killed there and the nun herself was taken prisoner and put into a man's bed.

Ruthless, even for the twelfth century.

In the next seven or eight years, MacMurrough managed to establish himself as king of Leinster, but there were discontents. The great north-Leinster families who had once held the kingship – the O'Tooles, Mic Faeláin and Mic Gillamocholmóc – regarded MacMurrough and his predecessors as usurpers, and since he tended to advance lesser men, very likely considered him a tyrant as well. In 1141, with O'Brien of Munster poised on the western borders of Leinster and O'Connor of Connacht about to have his armies marching all over Ireland – and both of them dangerous to MacMurrough – the discontented dynasts revolted. MacMurrough defeated them and exacted terrible vengeance: he blinded or executed seventeen of the leading Leinster dynasts and this, as the annalist observes, 'brought all Leinster under hand'. Now that he was firmly in the saddle in Leinster, he was able to fish more effectively in interprovincial waters, where he had already shown interest.

The best of spoils were to be had in the kingdom of Meath – and MacMurrough was not the only interested party. Turlough O'Connor, king of Ireland, attacked Meath in 1143, deposed its king, and appointed his own son, Conor, king of Meath. The Meathmen killed him within six months. Turlough led a great army into Meath and inflicted a slaughter on them 'like unto the day of doom' (as the annalist says) and divided up Meath: over west Meath he appointed one of the local dynasty as a puppet ruler: and he divided east Meath equally between Tigernán O'Rourke and MacMurrough. This settlement did not last long, but it gave MacMurrough a taste for territory in Meath and made him a bitter rival of Tigernán O'Rourke.

O'Rourke, whom, as we have seen, MacCurtain quaintly described as a 'virtuous holy man, and warlike withal', was ruthless even in twelfth-century terms – a fickle friend and a dangerous enemy. When he was party to an attack on Leinster in 1127, the annalist observes that 'the evil repute of that expedition lay upon Tigernán O'Rourke'. It was now his turn to be dealt with. In 1152, Turlough O'Connor and his new arch-rival, Murtough MacLoughlin, met near Beleek and made a solemn treaty of peace and friendship. Then the two over-kings and MacMurrough held a meeting in Meath which restored that kingdom to its proper ruler. Evidently, O'Rourke was not pleased by these developments and the allies turned on him, invaded his territory, burned his fortress, and set up a rival in his place. On this occasion, MacMurrough made off with O'Rourke's wife, Dervorgilla – and her goods and chattels – adding personal to political insult, and there is little indication of a romantic interest in the Irish sources. At any rate they were past the age of youthful passion. As Denis Taaffe put it in his *Impartial History of Ireland*, published in Dublin in 1811:

As the downfall of Troy was immediately occasioned by female lubricity, though without that cause it must have fallen under the dominion of the Greeks, so Ireland had its Helen captivated not by a buxom youthful Paris, arbiter of celestial beauty, but by an athletic grey-beard, Dermot MacMurrough, king of Leinster.

O'Rourke did not forget this – and settled the score thirteen years later. Evidently she returned to O'Rourke a year later – with her property – and the return was negotiated by O'Connor. And MacMurrough and O'Connor, despite severe pressure from

MacLoughlin, were to remain firm allies. O'Rourke naturally backed MacLoughlin, at least for the time being.

Early in the summer of 1156 the great Turlough O'Connor died in his fortress of Dunmore in Galway and his son Rory succeeded him. Rory had all the ambitions of his father, but less of his father's ability and energy. Two clear rival camps began to emerge in Irish interprovincial politics, that of O'Connor and that of MacLoughlin, and their struggles were to dominate Irish affairs until the Anglo-French invasion. O'Rourke allied with O'Connor, MacMurrough with MacLoughlin, and I doubt whether he had any higher motive than increased prestige and plunder as the supporter of the most powerful king in Ireland. But he was not simply a supporter: MacLoughlin came with the forces of the north into Meath and Leinster. MacMurrough submitted to him and handed him over hostages for Leinster and MacLoughlin made him a formal grant of the kingdom of Leinster – and this was the first of such formal grants.

Almost immediately O'Rourke and MacMurrough were at loggerheads over Meath, and O'Rourke was by far the more successful. Meath and north Leinster (including Dublin and the surrounding area) had become the key to the domination of Ireland – and as a result the cockpit of Ireland as the declining dynasties of Meath were set upon from every side.

MacMurrough now began to concentrate on the Ostman cities over which he already had some kind of authority as king of Leinster. In this MacLoughlin helped him. In 1161 he defeated the Ostmen of Wexford, but this was a mere beginning. Next year, helped by MacLoughlin, MacMurrough forced the Ostmen of Dublin into submission (after a tough struggle in which MacLoughlin got a bloody nose), and in the words of the annalist 'he plundered the Ostmen and obtained great sway over them, such as was not obtained for a long time'. There was relative peace in Ireland in 1163 and 1164, when MacLoughlin was at the height of his power.

His fall was swift and dramatic – the result of his own treachery towards one of his sub-kings, which caused revulsion throughout Ireland. With his fall, Rory O'Connor, O'Rourke and their followers moved with great speed. They marched first – and significantly – on Dublin where the Ostmen submitted and recognized O'Connor as king of Ireland, then to Mellifont to take the submission of Airgialla, and then they turned south into

Leinster against MacMurrough. They routed MacMurrough and he burned Ferns on their approach. Then he attempted to negotiate terms but, as the *Annals of Tigernach* (a Connacht source) put it crisply, 'he received no glory but the corpses of Uí Chennselaig'. Still, he was down, but not out. He could recover, if the dynasts of Leinster stood by him. They did not. The Ostmen of Dublin joined with the Leinstermen and together revolted against MacMurrough 'because of his crimes', say the *Annals of Tigernach*. And now it was the turn of the long-suffering king of Meath to invade Leinster. O'Rourke, too, could now settle his score. Quite apart from the matter of Dervorgilla – thirteen years before – there was the long-standing rivalry over Meath. Indeed, MacMurrough had inflicted a crushing defeat on O'Rourke in 1156 from which O'Rourke barely escaped with his life. They now joined with the Ostmen and the rebellious Leinstermen, marched unopposed into Uí Chennselaig, levelled MacMurrough's stone house at Ferns to the ground and expelled MacMurrough from the kingship. Clearly, the successful revolt of the Leinstermen was the principal cause of MacMurrough's ruin. So too Giraldus, who says:

The men of Leinster, seeing that their prince was now in a difficult position and surrounded on all sides by his enemies' forces, sought to pay him back, and recalled to mind injustices which they had long concealed and stored deep in their hearts. They made common cause with his enemies and the men of rank among this people deserted MacMurrough along with his good fortune.

O'Connor and his allies were so successful that nowhere in Ireland could MacMurrough look for help in the early summer of 1166, and evidently what enemies O'Connor had, found no use for a dispossessed king of Leinster – at least for the moment. Accompanied by his wife, daughter and a small number of followers, on or about 1 August 1166 MacMurrough sailed for Bristol from the south coast, to seek help abroad. A faithful follower of his wrote in the *Book of Leinster*:

O king of heaven, great the deed done in Ireland to-day [i.e. 1 August] i.e. the expulsion overseas of Diarmait son of Donnchad son of Murchad, king of Leinster and the Ostmen, by the men of Ireland. Alas, alas, what shall I do?

The details of his dealings with Henry II and his Anglo-French allies are well known and will only be told in summary here. MacMurrough and his party were received by the reeve of Bristol, Robert fitz Harding, a trusted confidant of Henry II, and very likely it was he who tactfully advised MacMurrough to approach Henry II who was then busy with his French dominions. MacMurrough crossed to France and it was some time before he managed to catch up with Henry. Henry apparently received him affably, MacMurrough took an oath of fealty and in return Henry granted him letters-patent to the effect that he had taken his vassal, Diarmait, prince of Leinster, into his favour and had empowered him to seek help anywhere within his dominions. This was little more than a licence to recruit freebooters. MacMurrough returned to Bristol, had his letters-patent read publicly, and made liberal promises of land and pay to anyone who joined him. For a while his offers were not taken up but, eventually, MacMurrough was approached by a great man somewhat down on his luck: Richard de Clare (known to Irish history as Strongbow) earl of Striguil, a marcher lord who had lost much because of the successes of the Welsh and because he had been hostile to Henry II. A bargain was struck between the two: MacMurrough gave Strongbow his daughter Aoife in marriage and the right of succession to the kingdom of Leinster on his death, and Strongbow agreed to come to MacMurrough's assistance the following spring. While Strongbow temporized MacMurrough found two further allies: Robert fitz Stephen and Maurice fitz Gerald, old feudal connections of Strongbow's family. MacMurrough promised these two adventurers the town of Wexford and the two adjoining cantreds as a fief if they came to Ireland 'with the westerlies and the first swallow' – late spring or early summer of the next year. Early in August 1167 MacMurrough sailed for Ireland, from St David's, with a small band of Anglo-French knights and archers. He was well received and was soon reasserting his claim to be king of Leinster.

Meanwhile Rory O'Connor had gone from strength to strength and shortly after MacMurrough's return he marched with his allies into Leinster. MacMurrough submitted to O'Connor and handed over hostages. He also paid O'Rourke a hundred ounces of gold in compensation for the wrong done him, and O'Connor withdrew leaving MacMurrough king over his territory of Uí Chennselaig. Throughout 1168 MacMurrough lay low, awaiting help from overseas.

In May 1169 two small Anglo-French bands, led by Robert fitz Stephen and Maurice de Prendergast, landed at Bannow Bay and soon made contact with MacMurrough, who joined forces with them, and together they marched on Wexford. After a brief resistance the city surrendered and MacMurrough granted it and its lands to his new allies. Now MacMurrough's prestige rose quickly again and many of his former enemies made their peace and joined forces with him, but north Leinster and Dublin held aloof. At this point, O'Connor and his allies marched into Leinster and began negotiations with MacMurrough. An agreement was finally patched up through the good offices of the clergy: MacMurrough was left his kingdom of Leinster but he undertook to acknowledge O'Connor as king of Ireland and handed over his son, Connor, as a hostage. There was a secret clause, too, according to which MacMurrough was to bring no more foreigners into the country and get rid of those he had as soon as Leinster was reduced to obedience. Apparently he had no intention of keeping he word. His ambitions grew with the prospect of success, and now that he was again king of Leinster – if only precariously – he dreamt of becoming king of Ireland with Anglo-French help. And with this in view he sent messengers to Strongbow urging him to hurry over to Ireland. Strongbow, who was playing a cat-and-mouse game with Henry II about permission to go to Ireland, was in no position to hurry, but he sent a young follower of his, Reimund le Gros, with a small troop. From the first coming of the Anglo-French until the arrival of Strongbow, MacMurrough remained firmly in control of his new allies and all major decisions were taken by him. He simply used his allies to maintain and expand his old authority as king of Leinster. With the arrival of Strongbow control passed largely into Anglo-French hands.

Strongbow sailed from Milford Haven and arrived in Ireland on 23 August 1170 with two hundred knights and a thousand other troops. Reimund le Gros joined him and two days later they attacked the city of Waterford which was defended by its own citizens and the Irish lords of the region. MacMurrough arrived – with fitz Stephen and fitz Gerald – some days after the bloody taking of the city. He confirmed his agreements of 1166 and Aoife and Strongbow were married in Waterford. Strongbow and MacMurrough now decided to attack Dublin. Its ruler alerted O'Connor, who marched to Dublin and encamped at Clondalkin to the south-west of the city awaiting the arrival of MacMurrough and his Anglo-French. They avoided O'Connor's troops by marching through Glendalough and over the mountains. Negotiations were opened between the three parties in which Laurence O'Toole, archbishop of Dublin, played a leading part. While talks were going on the Anglo-French suddenly attacked the city, took it, and set fire to it. Dublin fell on the feast of St Matthew, 21 September 1170. O'Connor struck camp and marched home. This left Dublin to MacMurrough and his allies and even allowed them to plunder deep into Meath and, later, to attack and defeat MacMurrough's enemies within and about Leinster. Now the vacillating king of Ireland, who was rapidly losing control of southern and midland Ireland, started new talks with MacMurrough and when MacMurrough refused obedience, the king executed his hostages – MacMurrough's son, his grandson and his foster-brother's son. Undeterred, MacMurrough pushed ahead on all sides as O'Connor's authority crumbled. Domhnall O'Brien, king of Thomond, now went into rebellion against O'Connor, and MacMurrough sent Robert Fitz Stephen and his knights to help O'Brien. This struggle dragged on until the winter and began again in the following spring.

MacMurrough saw little of the next year's campaigns. He died in his house at Ferns about 1 May 1171.

MacMurrough was something more than a turbulent and relatively unsuccessful twelfth-century Irish provincial king in an era when the kingship of Ireland was what was really at stake. He may have been trying to establish a new type of centralized authority over his own kingdom. This could explain his tyranny over his own over-mighty subjects, but he seems to have failed ultimately in this aim. In common with all the greater kings of the twelfth century, he realized that Dublin was the capital of Ireland – the power-base from which to control Ireland was the city and its hinterland within a radius of forty miles – but despite his best efforts he could not exercise effective control over it, and the Dubliners had their share in unhorsing him in 1166. Throughout his relatively long reign he played second fiddle in the political struggle, a star of the second magnitude.

Ironically, he did much for the Church, and here, what he did was appreciated. He helped to introduce the foreign orders of the twelfth-century reform. He founded the abbey of Augustinian nuns, St Mary's, in Dublin in 1146 and two convents of nuns in Carlow and in Ossory. In his own town of ferns he founded an abbey for the canons of Arrouaise about 1160 (and there he was buried in 1171). Some time after 1161 he founded the priory of All Hallows in Dublin (on the site of Trinity College) and the charter was witnessed by his brother-in-law, St Laurence O'Toole, and by Aed Ó Cáellaide, bishop of Louth, Diarmait's foster relation whom he describes as his 'spiritual father and confessor'. And, most important of all, he founded and generously endowed the great Cistercian abbey of Baltinglass in County Wicklow about 1148. This led to an appreciative letter from St Bernard – which is unconsciously ironic in more ways than one. It reads:

To the sublime and glorious king of Ireland ... we have heard of your glory in our country and we are overjoyed and delighted about all the good things we have heard about you, for you have received Christ's poor, or rather Christ in the form of the poor, with royal munificence. It is really a great miracle in our opinion that a king at the end of the earth, ruling over barbarous peoples, should undertake works of mercy with great generosity. ... Therefore we give thanks to your royal majesty and pray for you and for your health to the King of heaven that the Lord our God may grant peace in your days. So that you may more willingly and carefully finish what you have begun, we make you a participant in all the good works which are performed and will be performed in our house and in our whole order.

Flattery like that was worth a lot of land, and we should not make too much of MacMurrough's good intentions, nor see here the hand of a bold innovator, modernizer, or Europeanizer – as some have done. Twelfth-century kings manipulated the Church for prestige and power, just as the churchmen (witness Bernard) manipulated the kings for property and support – and in that, MacMurrough was one of the boys.

In his appeal to Henry II and to the Anglo-French he changed the course of Irish history – and he over-reached himself. He was soon out of his depth. He quickly lost control of his helpers whilst his ambitions raced towards the kingship of Ireland: he failed to grasp (or ignored) the anxieties caused by the very success of his Anglo-French allies to Henry II; and he died suddenly in 1171 at a critical time for the enterprise. The invitation inevitably became an invasion, and like most great changes in history it was an accident, unforeseen and unplanned, which opened Ireland to expansive Anglo-French feudalism – as England and Scotland had been opened. Ireland would have been drawn into that feudal world eventually, closer to its neighbour, and would have received feudal colonists, but no doubt in a different way. If MacMurrough wanted to make himself king over an Ireland of Gael and Anglo-French – like the type of kingdom that was emerging in Scotland under David I – he failed utterly, and in his failure brought down his own dynasty, and eventually the society which produced him. And I end, as I began, with another obituary – this time a sympathetic one, at the end of the list of the kings of Leinster in the *Book of Leinster*:

Diarmait son of Donnchad son of Murchad (reigned) 46 (years) and he was king of the southern half of Ireland and of Meath. He died at Ferns after the victory of unction and penance in his 61st year.

And his obituarist ends the list with an interesting comment from a sympathizer:

Thereafter, the English wretchedly rule. Amen. Amen.

FURTHER READING

There is no scholarly biography of MacMurrough, but there are several useful studies. F. X. Martin, *No Hero in the House: Diarmait MacMurchada and the Coming of the Normans to Ireland* (Dublin 1977) is a sympathetic historical and historiographical meditation on MacMurrough and the Anglo-French invasion. G. H. Orpen's *Ireland under the Normans* (4 vols. Oxford 1911-20, repr. 1968), i, pp. 39-100, 140-222, contains a detailed but relatively hostile account of MacMurrough and his politics. D. Ó Corráin, 'The education of Diarmait MacMurchada', *Ériu* 28 (1977), 71-81, treats of his youth and some common misconceptions about his education. Brian Ó Cuiv deals thoroughly with MacMurrough's nickname in Irish history in 'Diarmaid na nGall', *Éigse* 16 (1975), 136-44. F. J. Byrne, *Irish Kings and High-Kings* (London 1973, repr. 1987), pp. 272-74, makes interesting suggestion about MacMurrough in the context of the struggle for the kingship of Ireland. Nicholas Furlong, *Dermot, King of Leinster and the Foreigners* (Tralee 1973), is the fruit of considerable research and is written in an easy and popular style.

The reference to the *Annals of Tigernach* can be found in Whitley Stokes (ed.), 'The annals of Tigernach', *Revue Celtique* 18 (1897), 281, 268, 270. That to the *Annals of the Four Masters* in John O'Donovan (ed.), *The Annals of the kingdom of Ireland by the Four Masters* (7 vols. Dublin 1851), ii, pp. 1182-3 (*s.a.* 1171). That to the *Annals of Clonmacnoise* is in Denis Murphy (ed.), *The Annals of Clonmacnoise* (Dublin 1896), pp. 199-200. That to the *Annals of Loch Cé* is in W. M. Hennessy (ed.), *The Annals of Loch Cé* (2 vols. London 1871, repr. Dublin 1939), i, pp. 130-31. The citations from Giraldus Cambrensis will be found in A. B. Scott and F. X. Martin (eds and trans.), *Expugnatio Hibernica: the Conquest of Ireland by Giraldus Cambrensis*, New History of Ireland Ancillary Publications 3 (Dublin 1978), pp. 24-7, 40-41, 42-3. The quotation of G. T. Stokes is taken from his *Ireland and the Anglo-Norman Church* (London 1892), pp. 17-19 – a treasure trove of quaint Victorian moralizing. For St Bernard's letter, see G. -G. Meersseman, 'Two unknown confraternity letters of St Bernard', *Cîteau in de Nederlanden* 6 (1955), 173-8. For the lands granted by MacMurrough to Baltinglass see K. W. Nicholls, 'The charter of John, Lord of Ireland to the Cistercian abbey of Baltinglass', *Peritia* 4 (1985), pp. 187-206. The citations from the *Book of Leinster* will be found in R. Best *et al.* (ed.), *The Book of Leinster* (6 vols. Dublin 1956-83), i, pp. xvi, 184.

De Courcy entering Downpatrick. — Page 68.

III

JOHN de COURCY (c. 1150-1219) and the Medieval Frontier

JAMES LYDON

IN THE FIRST TWO centuries of the new millenium after 1000 Christian Europe expanded in all directions in a momentous series of adventures that changed the course of history. German colonization east of the Elbe pushed the Christian frontier in one direction, while at the other end of Europe Islam was driven back in the Iberian peninsula. At the heart of this forward movement were the Normans, pushing southwards into Sicily and Italy, eastwards with other Crusaders into the Holy Land, and most important of all northwards across the narrow channel into England. From England they expanded remorselessly into Wales, then Scotland, and eventually in the 1160s westwards into Ireland. To say that the arrival of the Normans on this island was next to the coming of Christianity in the fifth century, the most important single event in our history is no exaggeration. The men who led this invasion, who carved out lordships for themselves in Ireland, who forced the great Angevin King Henry II to follow them across the Irish Sea, so that Ireland as a result became permanently attached to the English Crown – these men became heroes, famous in history and legend subsequently. Richard de Clare, earl of Pembroke, better known to us as Strongbow, was made the subject of a Norman-French epic which we call *The Song of Dermot and the Earl* – 'Dermot' being the king of Leinster, Dermot Mac Murrough, whose daughter married Strongbow. But undoubtedly the most popular of all these adventurers to later generations, the man around whom the most fantastic legends were spun, was John de Courcy, conqueror of Ulster, who pushed the Norman frontier to its furthest limits in the north of this island. It was he, more than anyone else, who gripped the imagination of the later Anglo-Irish, so that they made him a symbol of their own independence and depicted him as a giant among men, fearless in battle and a champion of freedom. In the sixteenth-century *Book of Howth* he is thus described while fighting in Ulster:

He fought that day with a two-handed sword more like a lion than a lamb; his blows were so mighty and so to be wondered at that very strange it was to behold, for there was never a blow he struck but slew a man or two, for no harness could bear out his force ... Assuredly there was not a Tristan, Lancelot, nor Hector, that could do more than Sir John did that day ... He was one of the strongest men that then was in Europe. The valientest, the fairest the courtest, the soberest, the wisest, the fiercest in Europe was not his like.

He was like one of the great heroes of romance – a Hector, a Tristan, a Lancelot – all of whom were perfect knights in the best traditions of chivalry. Later admirers saw John de Courcy as representing all that was best in their ancestors, those heroic figures who conquered Ireland and established the English presence on the island. He was the man who carved out a principality for himself in the far north of Ireland, who defied the autocratic King John, and who represented all that was best in the self-confident, self-sufficient, independent adventurers who led the first English conquest of Ireland. Does the reality match the legend?

John de Courcy came from humble enough origins, unlike most of the others who invaded Ireland. He came from what might be called minor gentry in Somerset. He had worked his way up in the king's service, attached to his household and close enough to King Henry II to be the recipient of royal favour. He may have been with Henry in Ireland in 1172 when the king, according to the Norman-French chanson, *The Song of Dermot and the Earl*, granted him Ulster 'if he could conquer it by force'. By Ulster was meant not the modern province, but that part of it which lay east of the Bann in the modern counties of Antrim and Down. This was the old Irish Kingdom of Ulaid and it would have been wholly typical of King Henry to make a speculative grant of it, even in jest, despite the fact that its Mac Dunleavy king had made formal submission to him. At any rate, when de Courcy came to Ireland in 1176 with a small retinue of ten knights, he may well have had Henry's offer of Ulster in mind. According to Giraldus

Cambrensis, or Gerald of Wales, the contemporary historian of the English conquest of Ireland, the Dublin garrison at that time was behind in pay and highly discontent with their lot. They were ready for de Courcy to involve them in his enterprise. Twenty-two knights and three hundred other soldiers agreed to follow de Courcy in an invasion of Ulster, a mad adventure which seemed doomed to failure. If the force led by de Courcy was well up to the level of the retinues which followed the early invaders of Ireland, it was ridiculously small for what he now proposed to achieve. He left Dublin in the depth of winter, had to travel for three days through mainly hostile country, and eventually would have to fight an enemy which would hopelessly outnumber him. Norman advances had pushed into Meath and into north county Dublin, but beyond that lay unconquered, hostile land. The Treaty of Windsor of 1175 between Henry II and Rory O'Connor, the high king, had reserved the whole of Ireland, outside Dublin, Meath, Leinster and Munster from Waterford to Dungarvan, as Irish land, subject in theory to Rory and beyond the reach of land-hungry Normans. No wonder de Courcy's plan of conquering Ulster seemed mad.

According to Gerald of Wales, he had a famous prophecy in his favour, which foretold how 'a white knight, astride a white horse, bearing a device of birds on his shield, will be the first to enter Ultonia in a hostile invasion'. Since de Courcy was blonde, riding a white horse and had eagles painted as a device on his shield, he matched the prophecy and seemed to be the warrior who was destined to conquer Ulster. How could he lose, with such omens in his favour? It is true, as we shall see, that de Courcy believed in such prophecies, or at least pretended to, and actively encouraged the popular view that he was predestined to victory.

But in 1177, when he set out for Ulster, he needed more than prophecy to ensure victory. Yet against all the odds he won a success that can only be described as spectacular. First the cathedral city of Down was taken. Not even the presence in the city of the papal legate, Cardinal Vivian, inhibited de Courcy. He proceeded to fortify Down, won a series of battles against the local Irish and gradually gained control of the Irish kingdom of Ulster. Against overwhelming odds, de Courcy succeeded in carving out for himself a great lordship in Ulster. The legend of the military giant, virtually unstoppable, was born. De Courcy had proved himself to be a great soldier and an inspiring leader in battle.

Gerald of Wales describes vividly 'the blows dealt out by John's sword, how it lopped off now a head from someone's shoulders, or again arms and hands from their body' in one battle. On another occasion, after a raiding party led by de Courcy was defeated, so that only eleven knights were left alive with him, they

fought their way through to his castle, despite the fact that they had to cover a distance of thirty miles, over which they continually had to defend themselves against a large force of the enemy, without their horses, which had been lost, wearing their armour, on foot, and having had nothing to eat for two days and nights. Truly an amazing achievement and one which deserves to be remembered by posterity.

So wrote Gerald of Wales. And the praise seems well deserved.

At the same time we should remember that these Normans enjoyed a considerable military advantage over the Irish. They wore heavy armour while, as Gerald of Wales tell us, the Irish 'rode naked into battle', meaning that they wore no protective armour. The weapons used by the Normans, and in particular the fearsome longbow carried by their Welsh archers, which had an enormous range, rapid firing power, and the capacity to penetrate deep into any target unfortunate enough to be in the way, were all much superior to the less sophisticated weapons available to the Irish. But perhaps more than anything else it was the heavily armoured knight or man at arms, mounted on his huge warhorse, which struck terror into the hearts of the enemy. Irish annals reflect this fear, even later in the thirteenth century, when the appearance of the heavy cavalry was enough to cause the opposition to break ranks and flee. It took exceptional bravery to stand in open ground and face the charging knights. When the *Book of Mac Carthy* recounts the story of the first battle won by de Courcy in Ulster, it describes how the Ulaid 'retreated without striking a blow when they saw the Englishmen with their horses in full battle dress'. John de Courcy knew well how to exploit this advantage. His skill as a soldier and his qualities of leadership enabled him to emerge victorious against overwhelming odds. So his reputation as a great soldier in legend is well deserved and is based on the facts of history.

But John de Courcy was much more than a great soldier. In the second battle of Down, fought 24 June 1177, he was confronted by a formidable confederation of Irish, with the Ulaid led by Mac

Dunlevy, the Cenél Eóghan under Maelsechlainn Mac Lochlainn, and men of Airgialla there as well – fifteen thousand in all, according to Gerald of Wales, which is no doubt a great exaggeration, but is the writer's way of stressing how large was the force opposing de Courcy. But perhaps even more important, the coarb of Patrick (or the archbishop of Armagh) was also with the Irish, together with other clergy who carried a formidable array of precious relics which would protect the Irish and lead them to victory. According to the *Book of Mac Carthy*, however, the Irish 'fled without striking a blow, leaving behind Patrick's coarb with his clergy and the Canóin Pádraig'. Seven other important relics were abandoned, in addition to what are called simply 'many other relics'. The Canóin Pádraig is the manuscript now preserved in the library of Trinity College. which we know as the *Book of Armagh*. This was the most precious book formerly in the library of the monastery of Armagh, since it was believed to be an autograph of the great St Patrick himself, containing his confession as well as other writings. The *Book of Mac Carthy* describes how this precious relic, together with a famous bell, were 'brought back from the Galls, after they had been found in the slaughter, when their young keepers were killed. The Galls have all the other relics still.'

Like most men of his time, de Courcy was a firm believer in the power of relics and in returning the most valuable of them to Armagh he showed his statesmanship as well as his respect for ecclesiastical authority. He is nowhere mentioned in connection with the Bacall Íosa, of Staff of Jesus, venerated at Armagh for centuries as the very crozier given to St Patrick,as a symbol of his episcopal authority, by an angel sent by God. In a passage in which he describes the special veneration given in Ireland to the croziers and pastoral staffs of the saints, Gerald of Wales writes of the Bacall Íosa as the most famous of all. 'It was with this', he wrote, 'that according to popular belief that St Patrick expelled all venomous reptiles from the island. Its origin is as uncertain as its powers are most certain. This valuable treasure was transferred from Armagh to Dublin, in our day, and by means of our people.' It was preserved and venerated at Christ Church cathedral for centuries and it drew crowds of pilgrims from all over Ireland, until it was destroyed by the iconoclasts of the Reformation in the sixteenth century. There seems little doubt that its removal from Armagh to Dublin was part of a process which was designed to challenge the ecclesiastical primacy of Armagh and to establish Dublin as at least the equal of the northern see. To do this St Patrick would have to be given a close association with Dublin, where there was already a church dedicated to his name and a long-established cult, and where early in the thirteenth century a new cathedral was dedicated to him.

It was John de Courcy who championed Armagh and its claims to primacy against Dublin. No doubt this was done partly for political reasons, boosting his own claims to a measure of independence in Ulster. It was he who commissioned Jocelin, the Cistercian monk who came with others from Furness to establish a new foundation at Inch, to write the *Life of St Patrick* in 1186, to propagate the cult of the saint. Included in the *Life* is an episode which was designed to demonstrate beyond all doubt that Dublin was subject to the ecclesiastical authority of Armagh. According to Jocelin, Patrick converted the king of Dublin and with him all the citizens. The men of Dublin, in return for the gift of Christianity, 'by oath bound themselves and their posterity to the service of St Patrick and the primacy of the archbishop of Armagh', and Jocelin even included details of the tribute which they promised to pay. We know that the episode must be spurious. But the twelfth century reader did not. Historically, then, St Patrick had clearly established Armagh in a superior relationship with Armagh.

But de Courcy did much more than this to promote the name of St Patrick and the cult of the national saint. One of the first things he did after capturing Down was to import a community of Benedictine monks from Chester to serve the cathedral and changed its dedication from 'the church of the Holy Trinity' to 'the church of St Patrick'. He also changed the name of Down itself to Downpatrick. In the *Book of Howth* there is a story which tells how de Courcy later suffered the revenge of the Holy Trinity for this outrage. At the end of his days, when he was trying to return to Ireland, he had a dream in which he was told to abandon his journey. When he asked why, he was told that before the came to Ulster the church in Down was

in the name of Trinity Blessed ... and thou hast dedicated that church now to St Patrick; therefore God is offended with thee, and his pleasure is that thou shalt never (return) into that country that thou hast so much pleasure in, you that pulled down the master and put up the servant.

In one other respect de Courcy again attempted to 'pull down the master', this time the king of England, when he issued coinage in Ulster which substituted the name of Patrick (*Patricius*) for that of the king and which also carried the image of a bishop's crozier. Whatever the political significance of that coinage, it surely illustrates de Courcy's devotion to the apostle of Ireland. But Patrick was not the only Irish saint whose cult de Courcy promoted. It was, he, according to Gerald of Wales, who discovered the bodies of the two other great saints of Ireland, St Brigit and St Colmcille, together with that of St Patrick. The three bodies were discovered in Down, 'lying in a vault containing three recesses, the body of St Patrick lying in the centre and those of the other two on either side. John de Courcy was then governor and under his direction these three noble treasures were discovered, through divine revelation, and translated'. De Courcy also possessed a copy of the prophecies of Colmcille, written in Irish, which Gerald of Wales tells us he always 'kept by him as a kind of mirror of his own deeds'.

It seems clear, then, that de Courcy was exploiting these Irish saints and the prophecies of Colmcille to foster his own image as the predestined conqueror of Ulster. Yet he was also a munificent benefactor of the Church and we can hardly doubt that he was sincere in his devotion to those saints. Men in the twelfth century were rarely as cynical about their religion as some of their successors today. De Courcy transformed the religious life of Ulster. As we have seen he introduced Chester Benedictines to Downpatrick. From Carlisle he imported Augustinian canons regular and Crutched Friars, also into Downpatrick. Two more Benedictine houses were established by him at St Andrew in Ards and Nendrum. More important were the Cistercian foundations at Inch and Grey Abbey. To Carrickfergus he brought Premonstratensians from Dryburgh in Scotland. He was also an innovator. The first migration of the new Gothic style of architecture into Ireland was under his auspices. And it was he who was responsible for the first foreigner to be appointed to an Irish see, when in 1178 he procured the appointment of Bishop Reginald to the see of Connor in the northern part of his Ulster lordship.

This importation of monks and cannons was, of course, part of the policy of colonization which was to establish the earldom of Ulster and change the landscape of the north-east of Ireland.

Settlers were attracted with grants of land, many bearing names which survived the centuries – Logan, Savage, Russell, Hacket. There was a Scottish element, too, which anticipated later Scottish settlement in Antrim. It was de Courcy who built the first castles in Ulster. First came the mottes, which to this day still dot the landscape, like the motte and bailey at Dromore which is among the very finest in Ireland. But he left a more enduring mark with his two great stone castles, that at Dundrum which guards the approaches by sea and land to south Down, and the one at Carrickfergus which still dominates the area. Here de Courcy held court, ruling like a prince and exercising almost royal jurisdiction. To some observers among his contemporaries he was assuming the role of prince. When Jocelin wrote his *Life of St Patrick* he dedicated it to de Courcy, 'Prince of Ulster'. In England, a chronicler in 1197 used the same title, describing him as 'prince of the kingdom of Ulster in Ireland' and later even listed him among the rulers of the world! It is true that John de Courcy did sometimes behave as if he were kinging it in Ulster, issuing coinage, interfering in Irish politics, acting the part of kingmaker in Connacht, and generally behaving as if he were ruling an autonomous lordship. Yet some at least of his coins were struck with the goodwill of the lord of Ireland, who sent dies for the coins from Dublin to Carrickfergus. And de Courcy was sufficiently trusted by Henry II for him to act as justiciar, or chief governor, of Ireland for a time. Here we come to the real question about de Courcy: was he trying to assume the mantle of kingship in Ulster, or was he simply trying, as best he could, to survive on the frontier between the lands subject, however fitfully, to the authority of the king of England and those which were ruled under a different law, language and institutions – trying to survive between what official terminology so vividly called 'the land of peace' *(terra pacis)* and 'the land of war' *(terra guerre)*?

There is no doubt of de Courcy's ambitions. The Irish annals make it clear that he won many Irish to his side. He began to fight in the Irish way. Like most of the other adventurers who created lordships in the English fashion in twelfth-century Ireland, he had little choice if he wished to survive. He had to adopt the ways of Ireland. In 1179 the annals describe him raiding neighbouring Irish kingdoms and carrying off a prey of no fewer than four thousand cattle. When in 1197 he went on a hosting as far west as Derry and, as the annalist puts it, 'returned in triumph', he was acting in the tradition of earlier Irish kings in the heady politics of post-Clontarf Ireland.

Perhaps what caused most suspicion was his unlicensed marriage to Affreca, the Manx princess. Her father Godred was king of Man, as was her brother Ragnald later. This gave de Courcy access to the Manx fleet. Through his wife he could also claim relationship with the lord of Galloway in Scotland, to whose son Gilbert he gave extensive lands along the Bann, south of Coleraine, in 1197. More important, his wife was also related to Somerled, the lord of Argyle, who also possessed a fleet. To someone as naturally suspicious as King John, these alliances made de Courcy appear to be dangerously ambitious. We should remember that de Courcy had risen to power first under Henry II and both he and his son Richard I had turned a blind eye to his pretensions in Ulster. Not so King John. He quickly showed how sensitive he was to any seeming challenge to his royal prerogative.. What finally caused him to determine on de Courcy's downfall is not certain. There is some evidence that de Courcy failed, and may even have refused, to do homage for Ulster to the new king after his accession in 1199, with the implication that he ruled Ulster independently. It may be true, as well, that de Courcy had been indiscreet in making public reference to the murder of Arthur of Brittany by his uncle King John. Whatever the reason, the king decided to bring him down and in Hugh de Lacy he found a willing instrument. De Lacy was a younger man, more ambitious and even stronger than de Courcy. He got the earldom of Ulster as his reward. De Courcy had to leave Ireland and he died in obscurity in 1219. Before then, however, he seems to have regained the goodwill of the king, accompanying him on his expedition to Ireland in 1210, which ended with the expulsion of Hugh de Lacy and the confiscation of his earldom. He also seems to have enjoyed a substantial pension from the king.

But if he had dreamed of an independent Ulster, where he would rule as a prince, he had failed in his dream and later legend is false when it depicts him as successfully defying a despotic king. He may have created the earldom of Ulster, which transformed the north of Ireland, and that is surely sufficient achievement for any man. But he never achieved real independence, never became in fact *Princeps Ultoniae*, never established a dynasty of his own. If that was his aim, he failed, and became one of history's losers.

FURTHER READING

The story of John de Courcy was first told by Gerald of Wales. It may be read, in translation, in A.B. Scott and F.X. Martin (eds), *Expugnatio Hibernica (The Conquest of Ireland) by Giraldus Cambrensis*, esp. pp 175-81 (the extensive notes on pp. 331-5 are expecially important). The more elaborate, later legend is to be found in J.S. Brewer and W. Bullen (eds), *The Book of Howth*, pp 80-115. The best modern account is still in G.H. Orpen, *Ireland Under the Normans*, ii, pp. 5-23, 114-18, 134-44. A.J. Otway-Ruthven, *A History of Medieval Ireland*, pp. 58-9, 62, 73-5, is also useful. A more recent short account is by F.X. Martin in *A New History of Ireland* (ed. Art Cosgrove), ii, pp. 135-6. For his secular and ecclesiastical buildings see *An Archaeological Survey, County Down*, pp. 103, 119, 197, 203, 207ff, 267, 272-3, 279ff, 289; A. Gwynn and R.N. Hadcock, *Medieval Religious Houses: Ireland*, pp. 107, 108, 134, 135, 209, 211; T.E. Mc Neill, *Anglo-Norman Ulster*, pp. 6-14. His coinage is expertly examined by Michael Dolley, *Medieval Anglo-Irish Coins*, pp. 2-5.

E. CUZZPATRICK

IV

THOMAS BUTLER, earl of Ormond (1531-1614) and Reform in Tudor Ireland

CIARAN BRADY

To CHOOSE THE TENTH earl of Ormond as a representative loser of Tudor Ireland must appear at first sight to be deliberately perverse. In an era in which the lives of such great men as Kildare, Shane O'Neill, Red Hugh O'Donnell and the second earl of Tyrone ended in defeat and ruin, Ormond's career appears to have been one of remarkable and indeed unique success. Born in 1531, he succeeded to the earldom in 1546 while still a minor, but he was to spend the next sixty years of his life steadily increasing his power in Ireland and his reputation at court until he had established himself at the height of his career as the most influential subject in the Tudor kingdom of Ireland.

Black Tom Ormond (he acquired the sobriquet at court in the 1560s but was also known as Tomas Dubh in Ireland) was an exceptionally gifted and lucky man. Blessed by nature with a powerful physique, good looks and a charming if dissembling personality, favoured by an early education at the court of King Edward VI which gave him access to powerful connections he was to exploit all his life, Ormond enjoyed a cluster of advantages which few of his rivals in Ireland could hope to match. Yet at the time of his coming of age he was not without serious problems of his own.

Even within his own lordship certain tensions arising out of his family's recent history remained unresolved. In 1519 on the death of the childless seventh earl, Ormond's grandfather, Sir Piers Butler, had seized the earldom and all of its entitlements. His claim, though strong in law, was somewhat obscure and was immediately challenged by several Butlers and by the rising Henrician courtier Sir Thomas Boleyn. None could actually depose him; but Sir Piers was compelled to devote the rest of his life attempting to impose his authority over the leading branches of the Butler dynasty (Mountgarret, Cahir and Dunboyne) while persuading King Henry of the legitimacy of his title. In both aims he enjoyed considerable though not total success. The increasing assaults of the Kildare and Desmond Geraldines against both the Butlers and the representatives of English government in Ireland, which culminated in the rebellion of 1534-6, convinced both parties that a strong Ormond earldom was indispensable. Sir Piers's son James, who succeeded as earl in 1537, battened upon his father's achievements. He used the position of trust which Sir Piers had won with the king to undermine the pro-Geraldine English viceroy, Lord Leonard Grey, and he strengthened his position with the Butler collaterals occasionally by coercion but more generally by securing generous rewards of Crown lands and favour for them.

Yet the fragility of the house of Ormond's newly won status was exposed in 1546 when Earl James attempted to undermine Henry's favourite viceroy, Sir Anthony St Leger, in the same way as he had ruined Grey. The king was unimpressed by allegations of corruption and angered by what he saw as a Butler campaign to place a veto on the vice-royalty. Thus, after a cursory examination at court, Ormond was forced to retract and apologize. Almost immediately after he had done so, however, the earl and several of his companions were mysteriously poisoned while dining at Ely House in Holborn. It is idle to speculate as to the cause of Ormond's death: Earl Thomas certainly believed his father had been murdered, but no contemporary charges were made and no inquiry was carried out. Whatever its causes, the consequences of the ninth earl's sudden death were extremely serious. The destruction of the Butler leadership now matched that of the Geraldines a decade before. The two great feudal rivals were again made equal, and around all of the Butler territories in Leinster and Munster surviving Geraldines and their allies came out to settle old scores. Confronted by this general assault and without the protection of a strong earl, the various Butler groups began to shift for themselves, fashioning alliances for their own survival without regard to the general Ormond interest. As they did so the centrifugal tendencies of the lordship which had been kept in check only by the diplomatic skills of the last two earls began to take hold. While young Thomas remained confined at court, the complete eclipse of the earldom was prevented only by the timely but costly marriage of his widowed mother to the son of their great rival the earl of Desmond. In the meantime, while Butlers and Geraldines thus occupied themselves with the re-negotiation of local arrangements, the Dublin administration enjoyed the prospect of establishing a new political system in Ireland in which no great lord would be pre-eminent and all would be equally subject to the English king of Ireland.

It was under such inauspicious circumstances that Earl Thomas returned to Ireland in 1555 to reconstruct the fortunes of his house: and the extent of his success in overcoming such formidable obstacles is a measure of his personal achievement as earl. Within thirty years Ormond was to succeed not only in reasserting control over his own family and followers and in worsting the Geraldines, but in surmounting even the most serious efforts of the Dublin government to subordinate him to its will. By any obvious standards, then, Ormond would appear to have been not a loser, but a winner, a man gifted in every undertaking with the Midas touch, unable, even if he tried, to lose. Yet the fate of that mythical, greedy old king whom the gods had favoured with gold was, as everyone knows, loss. Glutted by a surfeit of success he was to become isolated and feared, frustrated in the most simple things, unable to satisfy even his most elementary needs. Concerning Ormond who died peacefully in his bed at the age of eighty-two, there was of course no overt tragedy. Yet his long life nevertheless reveals the deep irony of a career haunted by failure in the midst of success, not merely in spite of that success, but because of it.

Ormond began his campaign for the reconstruction of the Butler interest immediately upon his return to Ireland with a brief but acrimonious dispute over protocol at the Irish council board. Kildare, who had also been returned to Ireland as part of the government's plan to balance both houses against one another, expected to sit next to the viceroy as the descendant of former governors. Ormond objected, asserting *his* right to the privilege through inheritance from his father who had held it since 1537, and after a brief fracas Ormond won his case. The squabble was perhaps unseemly; but it was none the less laden with implication. For through it Ormond had signalled that he would resist any attempt to rank him below or even on a par with the old

Geraldine enemy, and that he intended to exploit his family's past service to the Crown in any way that would facilitate his ambition.

In his attempt to persuade the government that he deserved to take precedence over Kildare as the premier servant of the Crown, Ormond secured unexpected and unwilling assistance from Shane O'Neill who was then forcefully pressing his claim that he and not his half-brother Mathew should be recognized as heir to the earldom of Tyrone. Shane's demands had severely divided the English administration in Dublin and in Westminster. Some supported the viceroy, Sussex, in insisting that Shane should not be allowed overthrow existing legal settlements, but many others shared the view advanced by Kildare that the realities of power dictated a new agreement with Shane. The division presented Ormond with both a problem and an opportunity. Since even Elizabeth appeared to endorse Kildare's conciliatory strategy, Ormond could not be seen openly to oppose it. Yet he took full opportunity of Shane's repeated excesses to lend support to the punitive campaigns which the queen sometimes permitted Sussex to make against him. In practice, therefore, Ormond associated himself with the war party in Dublin while avoiding overt confrontation with the peace policy favoured at court. In 1564, however, when Elizabeth at last tired of temporizing with Shane and determined to destroy him, Kildare's consequent fall from grace became the occasion of Ormond's rise to prominence. He who had remained aloof from the bitter disputes concerning Shane was now openly celebrated by the triumphant military men as the one Irish subject who had truly understood Shane's disposition and could now be counted on to serve against him.

It was timely vindication and one which Ormond was soon to exploit. But even before then his undemonstrative support for Sussex's war-efforts had yielded important practical results. In return for his service and discreet financial support, Ormond had received a long series of favours and rewards which were in the viceroy's gift. New leases on monastic lands were made out to him, old leases were generously renewed and often converted into outright grants. Such largesse did much to compensate the earl for his trouble; but more importantly it demonstrated to friends and enemies alike that Ormond had access to special sources of royal remuneration. Family relations and factional allies shared in the benefits of Ormond's favour and others came to realize that the way to secure their objectives was to obtain the earl's commendation in advance. All of this contrasted sharply with those who depended on the Geraldines and in particular on the earl of Desmond. Lacking personal connections in Dublin or at court, Desmond saw his allies drift slowly away to one who could better answer their needs. But Desmond faced an even more direct threat from Ormond's manipulation of government favour. Several disputes concerning title to land in Limerick and Tipperary and to custom duties in Youghal and Kinsale remained outstanding between the two earls, and in each case Sussex had strongly advised the queen in Ormond's favour. The issue became critical in 1564 when the death of the countess of Desmond allowed Ormond to launch a series of additional claims for the return of his mother's dowry. With his own lordship under threat and several of his vassals refusing to pay him homage, Desmond allowed himself to be provoked into a full-scale battle with Ormond in which he was defeated and taken prisoner. Such a flagrant breach of the peace on the part of both earls demanded severe punishment; but in 1565 it seemed impossible that Ormond, who had served so well against O'Neill and who had after all surrendered Desmond to the Dublin government, could have been to blame for the affray. Instead Desmond was adjudged to be the guilty party and despatched on the queen's command to the Tower of London.

By 1565, then, Ormond had outmanouevered the Geraldines at both local and national levels. But the pace of his advance inevitably gave rise to the old Tudor suspicion that the Butlers, like the Geraldines, harboured over-weening ambitions of their own. Since the 1530s the Tudor government had sought to re-establish English law in Ireland not by military conquest, which was regarded as too costly and uncertain, but by reaching an accommodation with the great lords of the island who had established a political order of their own in their respective regions. Central to the success of this campaign for legal reform was the agreement of the great Anglo-Irish houses of Kildare and Ormond, whose influence in the country at large was immense, to take the lead in the process of political change. The Geraldines' rejection of this role was signalled in the rebellion of 1534, but the subsequent defeat and disarray of the house of Kildare rendered surviving Geraldines more amenable to the reform strategy. In the 1540s under the leadership of the thirteenth earl of Desmond they co-operated closely with the government of Sir Anthony St

Leger, using their influence to further his policy of surrender and re-grant. The house of Ormond, on the other hand, had given enthusiastic support to reform from the outset. Earl Piers had been more than happy to contribute to the suppression of the Kildare rebellion and thereafter the Butlers were in the vanguard of all further efforts to silence Geraldine dissent.

Yet Butler support for reform was in large measure self-interested, and though the earls of Ormond were willing to introduce administrative and legal changes into their lordship, they were ready at all times to oppose any viceroy whom they believed threatened their vital interests. Their attempt to resist St Leger, as we have seen, had been severely checked (it was St Leger, Earl Thomas believed, who had been behind his father's poisoning). But it was St Leger also who sought to re-establish political balance by having both the young earl of Kildare and the young earl of Ormond returned to Ireland together in 1555 to resume the reformist roles which had been laid down for them twenty years before. In the following ten years Kildare's political defeat and Desmond's collapse into lawlessness threatened once again to disrupt the reform scheme, and so in 1566 the new viceroy, Sir Henry Sidney, moved to restore the *status quo*.

He set about doing so by granting modest favour to Kildare and his followers, by protecting Desmond's interests as best he would and by encouraging some of Ormond's neighbours like the Fitzpatricks and the O'Carrolls to maintain their independence of the earl. He asserted his authority more directly, however, billeting soldiers, holding assizes in Kilkenny itself and making known his plans to abolish Ormond's jurisdictional liberty in Tipperary. Most seriously of all he supported the claims of the English adventurer, Sir Peter Carew, to lands in Carlow upon which the Butlers themselves had already encroached. The Butler response to Sidney's challenge was sharp. Like the Geraldines in 1534, Ormond's brothers rebelled in 1569, denouncing the viceroy and raiding the lands of those who supported him.

Their rebellion presented Ormond with a grievous crisis; yet from the beginning two factors counted heavily in his favour. First, at the time of the outbreak Ormond was not in Ireland but at court where over the previous four years he had carefully established himself as one of Elizabeth's closest personal confidantes (her faithful Lucas, she called him); and by 1569

Elizabeth trusted Ormond sufficiently to allow him return to Ireland to take control of the situation himself. Her decision seriously compromised Sidney's authority, but the governor's position had already been weakened by a second factor working in Ormond's favour. In rising his brothers had not acted alone, but had joined an existing rebellion raised by the Desmond Geraldines after the arrest of the earl. Sidney lacked the power to confront this dual challenge and was thus in no position to oppose Ormond's offer to deal with both problems at once. Having arrived, Ormond reversed the course of the war, persuading the rebel Butlers to change sides and to serve without pardon against the Geraldines. The rebellion lasted until 1573, but by 1571 Ormond had attained his most important objectives. During his service he was granted complete military authority in Munster, being allowed prosecute or to pardon rebels at will. And most importantly, his claim that the loyal Butlers had been provoked into rebellion by the reckless behaviour of the viceroy was accepted as the orthodox explanation of events at court.

The rebellion thus consolidated rather than weakened Ormond's position in several respects. It hastened the decline of the already discredited Geraldines, and allowed Ormond to make further encroachments on their dependants and allies in the country. Even the attainder of the brothers and the damage suffered by the branches of Cahir and Mountgarret in the rebellion served to strengthen the earl's standing, rendering these unruly elements suppliant and dependent upon his influence for their eventual rehabilitation. But most importantly the rebellion had allowed Ormond to outface the English govenor in a simple trial of strength that made clear which of them possessed real power in Ireland. In 1576-8 Sidney attempted a re-trial by seeking once more to abolish the liberty of Tipperary and to impose a military tax in Kilkenny, but on this occasion Ormond succeeded not only in forestalling the challenge but in securing the viceroy's premature and abrupt recall. Thereafter only the most rash of administrators dared openly to attack Ormond's status. Sir John Perrot did so briefly in the mid-1580s by reviving Sidney's taxation scheme, but he promptly abandoned the attempt when Ormond openly criticized him at court. By Perrot's time Ormond's position was in any case well-nigh unchallengable. For in the years 1579-83 the second Desmond rebellion had not only ruined the Munster Geraldines for ever, but confirmed Ormond

---

as the most effective defender of the Crown's interests in Ireland. In the midst of that rebellion the Dublin administration had strongly opposed Ormond's appointment as commander of all forces in Munster, but its own manifest inability to suppress the Geraldines without him simply confirmed Ormond's quiet insistence that he alone possessed the military and political power necessary to bring the rebellion to an end.

When he actually did so, at the close of 1583, Ormond had succeeded not only in defeating his rivals in the traditional factional game, but in the far greater ambition of transforming the nature of the system itself. For whatever their previous allegiance, those natives seeking protection from the encroachments of the English soldiers and adventurers now settling in large numbers in attainted lands in Desmond, Leinster and elsewhere in the island could look no longer to the Geraldines but to Ormond alone. Thus in the 1580s Ormond set about creating a new political configuration, deploying his power in Ireland and his influence at Westminster to protect those who accepted his patronage, to intimidate those who refused it and to frustrate the English administrators, soldiers and planters who tried to oppose him. This was the time also of the great re-organization of Ormond's estates, of the refurbishing of Kilkenny Castle and most symbolically of the construction of his country house at Carrick, opulent, unembattled and modern: an emblem of the manner in which the earl planned to exert his authority in the future.

Yet this apparently unqualified success obscured by its very completeness some profound weaknesses in Ormond's position. His undisputed victory over the Geraldines extracted no simple surrender from this group. Some amongst them accepted the reality of Ormond's hegemony and sought to secure relief from a timely recognition of his status. But many others, embittered by the experience of the previous forty years, were ready to reject in its entirety the order of allegiance to English law and the English Crown within which Ormond had established himself so completely. Thus even among those who temporized there were many who were prepared to join with the militant exiles in a radical war to expel the English presence and to restore the old feudal ways.

Ormond's worsting of successive English viceroys produced no simple result in Dublin either. There, the English administrators and soldiers were compelled to accept Ormond's superiority at court, but along with this recognition there grew a deep disillusion with the strategy of conciliation and co-operation which had been central to Tudor policy for Ireland in the past, and a growing conviction that sheer confrontation was the only way in which English authority could be established in the island. Thus, as with the Geraldines, their resentment against the earl was extended to a repudiation of the policy which he had so effectively exploited. For both groups the reasons underlying disillusion with the policy of Tudor reform were very different, but the focus of their bitterness was identical: the all-successful earl of Ormond.

In the midst of his success such resentments posed no immediate threat to the earl. Yet they were made more menacing by the one failure which Ormond himself was compelled to acknowledge: he was as yet without an heir. Though he had fathered dozens of bastards, the early breakdown of his first marriage through some dark conduct on the part of the earl robbed him of the chance to breed a legitimate heir while his estranged wife lived. Released by her death, Ormond married again in 1584, but though his second wife bore him three children, only one survived: and she was a girl. By the early 1590s, then, the prospect that Ormond would die without a male heir had begun to emerge as a distinct likelihood. His decision not to press for the restoration in blood of his brothers now began to tell against him; for on his death succession to the earldom would pass in law to his attainted brother Edmund as so revert to the Crown. The possibility that the earldom would thus be dismantled was immensely attractive to Ormond's enemies, the English administrators and the remaining Geraldines who would have no part of Ormond's system. But for many among the Butlers themselves the recognition that they stood only to gain from a re-division of a lordship which Ormond had done so much to improve was a powerful inducement to disloyalty.

In the early 1590s Ormond's future was beginning to grow clouded. Yet ironically the circumstances which precipitated his rapid decline were almost identical with those which had brought him so much success in the past. As the situation in Ulster deteriorated and doubts mounted about the loyalty of the earl of Tyrone, Dublin turned grudgingly to Ormond to ascertain Tyrone's intentions and to keep him at peace. Ormond as ever was confident of his ability to restrain Tyrone, because for many years he had cultivated Hugh O'Neill as a principal bulwark against

Geraldine influence in Ulster. Tyrone, he assured the government in 1594, was fundamentally sound; and even in 1598, when O'Neill was clearly leading the rebellion, he insisted that a two year-truce would allow him to restore order in Ulster. In that year, however, the battle of the Yellow Ford and Tyrone's extension of the war into the rest of Ireland made a nonsense of such predictions and catapulted Ormond into an acute personal crisis. Simultaneous rebellions in Munster and the midlands forced him to fight a hopeless war on two fronts. Military failure precipated domestic upheaval as many of the Butlers, and even the nephew whom Ormond had chosen as his heir, defected to the rebels. A desperate effort to secure Kilkenny by negotiating personally with the rebel O'Mores issued only in his abduction and in the humiliation of his being set out to ransom.

By then Ormond's value to the Crown had depreciated sharply. For this time he had failed in his principal obligation to keep his erstwhile friend at peace. His English enemies now charged him with conniving at the rebellion as they had once charged Kildare with conspiring with Shane O'Neill. The allegation was, of course, outrageous; yet in one sense it was not entirely untrue. For the man who had so successfully reconstructed Irish politics in his own interests, and who seemed on the brink of establishing himself as a figure of unparalleled influence in the island, was the last one to induce the equally ambitious Tyrone to accept his mediation. Whatever Tyrone aimed at, it is clear that any settlement which would have obliged him to Ormond as his saviour and patron was simply unacceptable. Ormond's intervention, then, had failed not merely to keep Tyrone from rebellion: it had actually impelled him toward it. For Tyrone, like the Irish rebels who followed him and the English servitors who opposed him, had also come to see that Ormond had outlived his usefulness through exceeding it.

The final years of the once-great earl were ones of continuing decline. With his ambitious political scheme now in ruins and without the ability or the opportunity to play the grand patron to other men, Ormond was forced to devote himself entirely to the extremely difficult business of securing the succession on his reconciled nephew, Theobald. But even in this he was to know failure. In 1613 Theobald died, and as the old earl struggled in the last year of his life to transfer his estate to yet another nephew, he encountered fatal and quite unexpected opposition from his own child Elizabeth, who had married and English planter against his command and now fought bitterly and successfully for a marriage portion which would cut the earldom in two. Neglected by the earl in his pursuit of a male heir, forced into an earlier and fruitless marriage, she too, like so many before her, was determined that Ormond would not succeed in this last effort to impose his will upon others. For Ormond, like King Midas, had in the midst of all his gains forfeited also the love of his daughter.

FURTHER READING

Although the materials for a biography are relatively rich, Ormond has not yet received the full-length study he deserves. There is a brief but unsatisfactory sketch of his life by Sidney Lee in the *Dictionary of National Biography*; Cyril Falls, 'Black Tom Ormond', *Irish Sword* 5 (1961-2), pp. 10-22, is more interpretative but perhaps overstates the importance of Ormond's friendship with Queen Elizabeth. Much further information on the Butler group as a whole can be extracted from the dense telegraphic prose of G. E. Cokayne, *The Complete Peerage* (rev. ed. 13 vols. London 1912-49) under the entries for Ormond, Cahir, Dunboyne and Mountgarret. Richard Bagwell, *Ireland under the Tudors* (3 vols. London 1885-90), devotes appropriate attention to Ormond's activities, and is generally over-sympathetic. The background to Ormond's conflict with Desmond in the 1560s is traced in George Butler, 'The battle of Affane', *Irish Sword* 8 (1967-8), pp. 33-47; and the circumstances leading to the revolt of the Butlers in 1569 are described in detail in J. Hughes, 'Sir Edmund Butler', *Royal Historical and Archaeological Society, Journal* series iv, vol. 1 (1879) pp. 153-92, 211-31. On Ormond's failure in treating with Tyrone see James Graves, 'The taking of the earl of Ormond, 1600', *ibid.* series ii, vol. 3 (1861), pp. 388-432. That Elizabethan hack, Thomas Churchyard, was hired to provide a glowing account of Ormond's service on behalf of the Crown in *A Scourge for Rebels* (London 1584), but the best contemporary estimate of the earl's real ambitions and abilities is to be found in Sir Henry Sidney's highly critical 'Memoir ... addressed to Sir Francis Walsingham', ed. H. F. Hore, *Ulster Journal of Archaeology,* series I, vol. 3 (1855), pp. 37-44, 91-9, 346-53; vol. 5 (1857), pp. 305-15; vol. 6 (1858), pp. 179-95.

V

BISHOP WILLIAM BEDELL (1571-1642)
and the Irish Reformation

AIDAN CLARKE

EMMANUEL COLLEGE, CAMBRIDGE, WAS founded in 1584 by a group of men, commonly called 'puritans', who dissented in certain respects from the form of protestantism adopted by the Church of England but remained in communion with it in the hope of changing it from within, and who wished to provide an alternative education for the ministry to that available in the traditional colleges. Trinity College, Dublin, was founded in 1592 by men, mostly Cambridge graduates, who held similar views and who aimed to create a puritan seminary in the guise of a university. William Bedell, the second son of an Essex farmer, entered Emmanuel at the age of thirteen in the year of its foundation: forty-three years later he became the fifth provost of Trinity.

This progression was almost as uneventful as it was appropriate. Bedell was the quintessential scholar-cleric. Seventeen years of study and teaching at Cambridge, culminating in the bursarship of his college and a doctorate in divinity, were followed by parochial appointments, first to Bury St Edmunds in East Anglia and then, in 1616, to the country living of Horringer in the same area. These years of pastoral work were combined with continued study, some writing, and constant learned exchanges with like-minded men in nearby Cambridge. Bedell was a formidably well-endowed scholar who was familiar with Hebrew, Arabic and Syriac as well as with the classical languages, and although he was widely read in contemporary theological and controversial literature, and unusually well informed about the Greek Orthodox tradition, his special concern was to use his linguistic skills in the study of both the Bible itself and the writings of the early Church fathers. The extent of his knowledge of the primary sources of Church history gave him an individuality which eluded the stereo-typology of his time. Although many of his views coincided with those of the internal critics of the Church, he regarded the issues in dispute as matters for research, reflection and informed discussion, and reached his conclusions without reference to religious politics. As often as not those conclusions were closer to the puritan position than to that of the Church establishment, but Bedell was no readier to follow opposition fashion than he was to conform to official orthodoxies. His was an independently informed faith, anchored in his confident control of all the available evidence, and he was too much at ease with the intellectual history of religion to mistake a debating-point for an eternal truth.

His life was a quiet one. With his wife and three children he enjoyed what he called 'a good seat in wholesome air, with a little parish in compass of my weak voice, and about a £100 a year', and he attracted no public notice. But he was well known to those who respected what he valued. Among them was that greater scholar, who similarly defied classification by combining in an individual mix views from different bands of the contemporary religious spectrum, James Ussher, archbishop of Armagh. It was Ussher who, after consultation with Cambridge friends, formally invited Bedell to accept the provostship of Trinity in 1627.

Twenty years previously Bedell's studious and pastoral routine had been interrupted by an equally unexpected invitation. In 1607 a number of chaplaincies in English embassies abroad fell vacant: the mysterious intricacies of patronage decreed that they should be filled by Emmanuel men, and Bedell found himself in Venice with Sir Henry Wotton, diplomat and wit, unremembered author of that most candid of job descriptions: 'An ambassador', he remarked, 'is an honest man who is sent to lie abroad for the good of his country.'

The services that Wotton had in mind for his new chaplain went far beyond the normal embassy round of ministering to English residents and visitors. Venice was in dispute with Pope Paul V; had recently been under interdict; seemed ready to ally itself with the Protestant side in European quarrels, and might even be prepared to convert political opposition to papal authority into religious defiance, and become Protestant. While Wotton attended to the politics of this situation, Bedell's brief was to explore the religious possibilities. He became friendly with the Servite friar who acted as prime theological consultant to the Venetians, Paolo Sarpi, and with an outspoken Franciscan opponent of papal claims, Fulgentio Micanzio, and was encouraged to find that, as he phrased it, 'for the substance of religion they are wholly ours'. He began to teach them English and to import Protestant theological works to provide the materials they would need if they were to set about creating a native Italian Protestant tradition. He became involved in moves to bring together a congregation of Venetians who were, he reported, 'already alienated in heart and tongue from Rome'. A confession of faith was adopted, and an Italian version of the Bible chosen; Bedell translated the Book of Common Prayer into Italian to provide a liturgical model. His undiplomatic offer to act as minister to the congregation was prudently declined, however, and progress halted for want of an alternative.

Bedell's strategy was clearly thought out. He wanted both to lead the influential dissidents towards an appreciation of Protestant theology and to create the nucleus of a Protestant congregation among those of their followers for whom an intellectual approach was inappropriate. From the outset, he realized that international politics had made the opportunity, and might remove it at any time. And so it happened: French pressures and Roman diplomacy prevailed, the Venetians withdrew their co-operation, and Bedell and his ambassador were recalled to England late in 1610.

He had learned a good deal in three-and-a-half years. As a pastor he had observed the Counter-Reformation Church at work and been impressed, against the grain of the austere tradition in which he had been formed, by what he described as 'their liberality and cost in the solemn setting forth of their service and adorning their churches', and he had drawn the conclusion, also against the grain, that men 'are led much more by shows than substance'. He had been impressed, too, by the systematic vernacular instruction in the catechism which ensured that the fundamentals were familiar to all. As a theologian he had come to understand that there were, within the Catholic fold – and prepared to remain within it, however restively – men who shared his interests, subscribed to his values, and earned his respect, and whom he recognized as fellow members of the elect of God, as men whom God had predestined for salvation.

These were ideas which challenged, and indeed threatened, the dominant assumptions of Trinity and the Church of Ireland. Trinity had been largely shaped by Cambridge graduates who were at odds with the Church of England, found the Church of Ireland more congenial, and set little value on the official norms of religious observance. What began as principle may very well have degenerated into laxness during the lengthy provostship of Bedell's lay predecessor, and Bedell found religion outwardly 'much neglected' at Trinity. When he conducted a communion service on the Sunday after he had taken his oath of office, it was with the aid of a table, cloth and napkin specially purchased for the occasion, for the last such ceremony had taken place eleven years before. There was no resistance to the stricter standards of observance that Bedell insisted upon. But his attitudes towards Roman Catholicism were less easy to accept. From the outset, the Church of Ireland had exhibited a pronounced tendency to emphasize those elements in Protestantism that were most distinct from Catholicism, and both its credo and its theology incorporated a hostility towards Catholicism more extreme than their English equivalents. Only a few years previously Bedell had been able to point out to a correspondent that the identification of the Pope with Anti-Christ 'is no part of the doctrine of our Church'. But what was true in East Anglia was not true in Dublin, for the Irish Articles of 1615 did assert that the Pope was Anti-Christ. Moreover, it was commonly accepted by Irish Protestants that salvation was impossible within the Church of Rome. Bedell made no secret of the fact that he accepted neither of these propositions, and he used every opportunity, it was noted, 'rather to contract the differences between Protestants and Papists than to widen them'. This was the behaviour, his most stubborn opponent shrewdly and insultingly observed, of an 'Italianated man'.

Although Bedell held that salvation was possible within Roman Catholicism, he was far from regarding that as removing the need to assist Catholics to perceive and renounce the errors of their Church. On the contrary, he upheld the Church's evangelical mission with an urgency that challenged local Protestant sensibilities. In the beginning, when the Church of Ireland was formally established in 1560, it was little more than a legal fiction. The Acts of Supremacy and Uniformity, in purporting to change the character of an existing Church and requiring clergy and laity alike to become Protestant, far outran the power of the government. Clergy and laity for the most part remained Catholic, openly or furtively according to circumstances, and a mixture of financial constraints, government impotence, political expediency and the shortage of reformed clergy impeded the advance of a Protestantism that was, in any event, unsure of its way forward. Most tacticians argued that the Irish were barbarians who must be brought to civilized obedience before they could become receptive to Protestantism, and that the Church must wait until state power could provide it with congregations, but there were others who insisted that Protestants should reach out to the Irish and help to save what souls they could. To the former the use of the Irish language to evangelize was a cultural contradiction: to the latter, it was no more than commonsense.

Trinity had hovered between these extremes. It had, of course, been founded in part to play a civilizing role, but it had also been designed to produce a Protestant clergy to minister to the needs of new English colonists, and that proved to be the chief concern of those who controlled its policies. In the early years an attempt was made to set up a Gaelic printing press, with the publication of a translation of the New Testament as its first priority, but the enterprise failed and the impetus died. Trinity's sole contribution to the conversion of the Irish was the education of a handful of native Protestants who returned to their districts to preach the word. It was the scale rather than the character of this effort that gave rise to criticism. In 1620 King James took the College severely to task and demanded that

some competent number of towardly young men already fitted with the knowledge of the Irish tongue be placed in the university, and maintained there for two or three years till they have learned the grounds of religion, and be able to catechize the simple natives, and deliver unto them so much as themselves have learned.

Bedell took King James further than his word. He set about learning Irish himself, procured a new College regulation providing for a regular Irish lecture and for Irish prayers in chapel on holy days, made special Irish language service books available, employed a native speaker to supervise pronunciation, and prompted a translation of the psalms as a forerunner to a full translation of the Old Testament.

Although this won official approval, and Bedell was swiftly elevated to a bishopric early in 1629, local ecclesiastical opinion was not so easily beguiled into disregarding the wider implications of what Bedell was doing. The tendency to see Protestantism and anglicization as inseparable had been reinforced in the years after the turn of the century when, increasingly, in the absence of sufficient numbers of locally bred clergy, the Church of Ireland had both confined itself mainly to tending to the spiritual needs of Protestant settlers and had recruited its bishops and clergy from England. To men such as these, the Church's mission fused the cultural with the religious, and the proposition that preaching Protestantism to the Irish in Irish was the same as preaching it to the Venetians in Italian was grossly mistaken.

Bedell's consecration, in 1629, as bishop of the combined dioceses of Kilmore and Ardagh certainly signified an interest in some quarters in seeing his approach put to the pastoral test. Both his dioceses were in areas of recent settlement, in Cavan and Longford, but, as he observed, 'our new plantation is yet raw, the churches ruined', and most of the inhabitants were Irish. Systematically, Bedell tried to reach them. He instituted a daily service in Irish, prepared an Irish catechism, pressed ahead with the translation of the Old Testament, produced a series of concise descriptions of the main doctrines of the Church in Irish, and sought to ensure through his visitations and his appointments that his clergy did not limit their ministry to those who were already English-speaking and Protestant. He quickly discovered, however, that the historically evolved situation of the Church created obstacles to what he wanted to achieve. His own position as bishop of two dioceses epitomized one problem, that of manpower shortage. He had only thirty-two clergy, most of whom held more than one living, and some many more, which gave them more duties than they could discharge, so that the minimal requirement, that divine service should take place in each parish each Sunday, could not be met. There was little that Bedell could do beyond setting an example: he divested himself of the bishopric of Ardagh to a reputable cleric who had the private means to be able to afford to take it, and tried to persuade and bully his clergy into reformative action: to relinquish pluralist positions, to appoint able curates, to achieve higher standards of perfomance. He recorded some improvement, but the problem of an entrenched clergy, too unsympathetic to Bedell's novel approach to be co-operative and too poorly paid to live from the income of a single parish, was intractable.

Further difficulties arose from the way in which the Church of Ireland was regarded by the Catholic community. They saw it, he soon realized, not as a body of belief, but as an instrument of exploitation, and his experience left him in no doubt that they were justified in doing so. Although the collection of tithes and dues for services which were neither wanted not rendered had something to do with this view, its major source was the activities of the ecclesiastical courts. At that time they exercised jurisdiction over a whole range of offences of a sensitive moral character and had a vital role in the probate of wills and the resolution of testamentary disputes. Even in favourable circumstances, in Protestant England, this gave rise to bitter tensions between Church and community. In Ireland matters were made worse by the fact that the Church courts were not under the control of the ecclesiastical authorities: they were managed by professionals whose interest was profit, whose fees were exorbitant and whose decisions were open to suspicions of corruption. Bedell entered into a lengthy and futile dispute, suspending his Chancellor for a time and hearing cases himself without charge, but vested interest proved too strong for him. Just as he could not transform his clergy into an effective missionary force, so he could not alter the repellent aspect that the Church presented to those whom he believed it to be the Church's duty to attract.

His approach, though it appealed to James Ussher, had never been well received by his episcopal colleagues, and it became more unwelcome as time passed. When he pressed, at a meeting of convocation in 1634, for the general provision of services in Irish, he was sharply reminded by a fellow bishop that what he proposed was actually unlawful by the terms of an act passed by the Irish parliament in 1542. By that time the official stance had altered. A new lord deputy, Viscount Wentworth, had coldly appraised the situation and concluded that the Reformation had failed because it had been mis-managed. Accepting that it was senseless to purport to oblige everybody to attend weekly services when in most places no such services were provided, Wentworth devised a new strategy. The first essential was to make the Church of Ireland ready to receive and serve the whole community. Its finances must be strengthened, its churches re-furbished, the quality of its clergy improved and their numbers greatly increased. Only when this process was complete could uniformity be enforced effectively. Wentworth did not shrink from the corrollary, that in the meantime Catholicism should be allowed a practical toleration. In short, with greater analytical clarity, greater energy and administrative skill, and with a new ruthlessness towards opposition and vested interest, Wentworth came down in favour of that side of the Elizabethan argument which had held that the way forward was through systematic and comprehensive state action directed towards the community as a whole, rather than through missionary zeal, persuasion and the conversion of individuals. He wanted his bishops to be efficient, business-like administrators, undertaking the fundamental task of preparing the material basis for future action.

This was not an ethos in which Bedell was comfortable. He saw his duties as pastoral and drew his guidelines from his intimate knowledge of the primitive Church. And he went his own way: clashing with the lord deputy when principle required it; regretting that James Ussher had proved more yielding than himself; wrestling in private and in friendly correspondence with such matters as the nature of grace and the efficacy of the sacraments; seeking always to preach the word of God to those who had not heard it; embodying that minority tradition in the Church of Ireland which insisted that the religious vocation had to do with saving souls, not with resource management, capital accumulation and book-keeping.

There was to be no time to test the constructive value of Wentworth's gradualist strategy. In October 1641 the Ulster Irish rose in arms, put Protestants to flight and seized their property and churches. In the midst of much confused violence Bedell remained unmolested for two months, during which he turned his palace into an asylum for refugees, offering material and spiritual comfort, and disregarding warnings to desist. Briefly he was imprisoned in Cloughwater Castle, then released and allowed to live in the house of one of his Irish clergy, Denis Sheridan. That too was to be brief. On 4 February 1642, in his seventy-second year, Bedell died. The Church authorities, now Catholic, denied him burial in Kilmore. None the less, a fearfully defiant funeral procession bore his body towards the churchyard. Before they reached it, they were met by a contingent of rebels who, as Bedell's son later recalled, commanding their drum to beat, as the manner is when a soldier is buried, and placing the musketeers before the corpse, conveyed the bishop to his grave. And being come thither, the sheriff told the bishop's sons that they might use what prayers or what form of burial they pleased; none should interrupt them. And when all was done, he commanded the musketeers to fire a volley of shot, and so the company departed.

Twenty-three years later, when Ireland was quiet again, the Elizabethan Act of Uniformity was replaced by a new statute which acknowledged the existence of varieties of religious belief within the community. Membership of the Church of Ireland ceased to be a universal obligation and became a privileged status. That was a natural step for a Church that had been all-inclusive by law but exclusivist by preference, but it was not a step along the way that had won Bedell the respect of Irish Catholics.

FURTHER READING

E. S. Shuckburgh (ed.), *Two Biographies of William Bedell* (Cambridge 1902), is a good collection of primary materials which includes an extensive selection of Bedell's letters as well as accounts of his life by both his son and son-in-law. The Venetian episode may be traced in L. P. Smith (ed.), *The Life and Letters of Sir Henry Wotton* (Oxford 1907); Bedell published a Latin translation of Sarpi's *History of the Venetian Interdict* (Cambridge 1626). His writings have not been collected. The context within which he worked in Ireland is provided by Alan Ford, *The Protestant Reformation in Ireland, 1590-1641* (Frankfurt-am-Main 1985), and R. Buick Knox, *James Ussher, Archbishop of Armagh* (Cardiff 1967). The sixteenth-century background has attracted a good deal of attention lately, of a rather argumentative kind: the result has been to dispose of old interpretations without establishing new ones. The essentials of the debate are stated in Brendan Bradshaw, 'Sword, word and strategy in the reformation in Ireland', *Historical Journal* 21 (1978), and Nicholas Canny, 'Why the reformation failed in Ireland: une question mal posé', *Journal of Ecclesiastical History* 30 (1979). Karl Bottigheimer, 'The failure of the reformation in Ireland: une question bien posé', *Journal of*

Ecclesiastical History 36 (1986), summarizes the issues clearly and makes informed use of Bedell's experience in developing his own case. Canon G. V. Jourdan, who dealt with the Reformation period in W. A. Phillips (ed.), *History of the Church of Ireland* (3 vols. Oxford 1933-4), was ahead of his time in seeing ambiguities where others saw certainties, and his sixteenth-century chapters have not been altogether superseded. The most recent appraisal is Aidan Clarke, 'Varieties of uniformity: the first century of the Church of Ireland', *The Churches, Ireland and the Irish: Studies in Church History* 35 (Oxford 1989).

S. Harding delt.   W.N. Gardiner sculpt.

TALBOT, DUKE of TYRCONNEL.

From an Original Picture in the Collection of Lord Beaulieu at Ditton Park.

Pubd Novr 1. 1794. by E & S Harding. Pall Mall.

VI

RICHARD TALBOT earl of Tyrconnell (1630-91) and the Catholic Counter-Revolution

JAMES McGUIRE

THE PHRASE 'PROTESTANT ASCENDANCY' is first used in the later decades of the eighteenth century but the reality it describes is a product of the 1650s. For it was in this decade, the years of Cromwellian rule, that a revolution in land ownership occurred, a revolution which transformed Irish politics and society for the next two centuries. While the population of Ireland remained predominantly Catholic, political power and social standing, so closely linked in the seventeenth century to the ownership of land, were now Protestant preserves. The crude statistics of land ownership reveal the scale of this revolution. In 1641 almost 60 percent of the land was owned by Catholics; by the late 1660s, and despite the collapse of the Cromwellian regime and the restoration of the Stuart monarchy, just over 20 per cent of land was in Catholic ownership, a downward trend that continued well into the eighteenth century.

Accompanying this massive shift in ownership, indeed anticipating it, was an even more far-reaching transformation of political life. In 1640 about one-third of the members of the Irish House of Commons were still Catholic; some twenty years later, when the 1661 parliament met in Dublin, it was for all practical purposes an exclusively Protestant assembly, representative of both the longer-established Protestant landowners and the recently arrived Cromwellian settlers. And so the Irish parliament had become, what it was to be throughout the eighteenth century, a Protestant legislature.

With hindsight the historian can see that the 1650s marked a decisive turning point for the Catholic gentry and the newer Protestant landowners: for the former political and social obscurity, for the latter a social and political ascendancy that would last well into the nineteenth century. But hindsight can be deceptive for it confers on the past an appearance of inevitability which contemporaries never took for granted, be they Catholics who sought a return to their former social and political prominence, or the new Protestant gentry who feared for the security and stability of their Irish estates. Indeed for a brief period in the late 1680s, in the reign of James II, it looked as though the changes wrought by the Cromwellian settlement might well be overturned and the older Catholic gentry restored to their former political and social prominence. If this had happened credit or blame would in large measure have rested with James II's lord deputy of Ireland, Richard Talbot, earl of Tyrconnell, the only Catholic to be viceroy of Ireland in the centuries after the Reformation.

Richard Talbot (or Dick, as he was generally referred to by his contemporaries in the army and at court) was born in 1630 into a prominent Catholic family. His father, Sir William Talbot, was a lawyer and landowner and in 1613 member of parliament for County Kildare. Sir William was a typical member of the old Pale gentry, those who referred to themselves in the early seventeenth century as 'Old English', thereby distinguishing themselves from both the Catholic Gaelic Irish and the Protestant new English settler. Richard was the eighth of Sir William's eight sons, his eldest brother Robert succeeding to the baronetcy and playing a prominent part in Catholic politics in the 1640s. More significant was another of Richard's elder brothers, Peter Talbot, for a time a Jesuit priest and later Catholic archbishop of Dublin.

With a family background such as this it is hardly surprising that Richard grew up imbued with the values of the Catholic gentry and devoted to defending their social position. By the time he was twelve the defence of that position had forced the Talbots and other old English families into a political and military alliance with their Catholic co-religionists, the Gaelic Irish, in the Catholic Confederacy of the 1640s against the growing threat of a new conquest of Ireland by the puritan English parliament. Initially too young to be engaged in the fighting, by 1647 he was serving as a cornet in Preston's Catholic army and later, in 1649, in the defence of Drogheda against Cromwell's army, where he was seriously wounded and fortunate to escape. In the early 1650s, with the

Worsted in the Game

collapse of the Catholic and royalist cause in Ireland, like so many other Catholic officers Richard sought employment in Europe in the armies of Spain and France. Unlike many of these exiled officers, however, his contact with Ireland was far from over and he was to rise to a pre-eminence some thirty years later which could not have been predicted in the unpromising years of exile in the 1650s.

How was this eighth son of an Irish Catholic baronet saved from obscurity to become a prominent figure in the Restoration court and ultimately one of the most formidable viceroys of Ireland? The crucial moment in Talbot's career occurred in the 1650s in Flanders when his brother Peter, the Jesuit, introduced him to James, duke of York, brother of the exiled Charles II. It was the start of a long-standing friendship, one which would bear fruit politically in the later 1680s when the duke, by then a Catholic convert, succeeded his brother on the throne as James II. But even in the 1650s Talbot's new prominence was soon apparent with his appointment as commander of the duke's regiment. From this time onwards his career was intimately linked with that of this royal patron and friend.

It seems clear that Talbot soon established his influence over the duke of York and became the dominant partner in the friendship. He must have seemed a lively, personable companion to the young duke, with his propensity for duelling, women and military life (including an apparently reckless sortie into England for the purpose of attempting the assassination of Oliver Cromwell, which led only to his arrest and escape back to the Continent). Three years the duke's senior and with a domineering personality to which all his contemporaries bore witness, Talbot clearly knew just how susceptible James was to his influence and advice. For the remainder of his life he used this influence to serve his own interests and those of his countrymen, the 'old English' Catholic gentry of Ireland.

In 1660, when the commonwealth collapsed and the monarchy was restored, Talbot travelled to England and became, quite predictably, a prominent member of the duke of York's household. It is a measure of the importance of the Talbot family, and in particular of Richard's personal influence at court through his friendship with the king's brother, that the Talbots received far more considerate treatment in the Restoration land settlement than did most of the Catholic gentry who had been dispossessed or transplanted under Cromwell's government. It was they whom Richard now sought to serve in the shaping of the land settlement.

The problem faced by the Catholic gentry seeking restoration of their estates in the 1660s was the government's relative powerlessness to undo the Cromwellian settlement to any great extent and to restore them to their estates. The fact of the matter was that the beneficiaries of the Cromwellian settlement were *in situ* in Ireland; for the government to disturb them in their estates would be to run the danger of provoking them into armed resistance with all that that would imply for the stability of the restored monarch not just in Ireland but in England also. So while the king and his ministers (especially Ormond and Clarendon) may have been better disposed towards the Catholic gentry than the Cromwellian settlers, reasons of state, indeed common prudence, required that the Cromwellian settlement should remain substantially intact with the Catholic gentry regaining only a modest restoration of what they had enjoyed in 1641.

The restoration land settlement was incorporated in two statutes passed by the all-Protestant Irish Parliament: the 1662 Act of Settlement and the 1665 Act of Explanation. For Irish Protestant landowners these statutes were the fundamental guarantee of their estates and position in Ireland. Any attempt to whittle away their provisions, worse still to suggest that they were not the last word on the land settlement, created anger and alarm in Protestant Ireland. This Protestant determination to preserve the integrity of the settlement was matched quite predictably by a Catholic desire to see it substantially modified or even repealed. In the vanguard of attempts to undo the settlement was the duke of York's friend and adviser, Richard Talbot. Of those Catholics who regained some of their lands in the 1660s, a number undoubtedly owed their good fortune to Talbot's efforts on their behalf, particularly his lobbying of the king and his ministers when the details of the settlement were being drafted.

But it was not until 1670 that Talbot became the leading actor in a sustained effort at having the whole question of the land settlement re-opened. A formal request from fifty-eight Catholic gentlemen to represent their interests at Whitehall provided him with the necessary credentials to seek amelioration. The political climate in 1670 was also propitious since Charles II was embarked upon a concerted attempt to introduce major changes in government policy: religious toleration, a pro-French foreign policy, a secret commitment to Louis XIV to support Catholicism in his dominions, and a general determination to assert the royal prorogative. It was certainly an auspicious time for Talbot to seek a review of the land settlement and the opportunity was not lost. Over the next two years government committees presided over by Prince Rupert, the king's cousin, took evidence from the aggrieved, heard submissions from Talbot and his counsel, and discussed the feasibility of altering the settlement.

At any time these deliberations would have been worrying to the protestant landowners of Ireland but the fact that they were talking place at Whitehall while Charles II's viceroy in Ireland, Lord Berkeley, was turning a benevolent eye towards the activities of the Catholic clergy, disturbed not just Irish Protestant landowners but those politicians in England who strongly opposed the king's foreign and domestic policies. By early 1673 the English parliament was taking a keen interest in royal policy towards Ireland largely because of its implications for England. This resulted in a formal parliamentary address to the king asking that Prince Rupert's enquiry commission into the Irish land settlement be abandoned, that Catholic office-holders be dismissed and the Catholic clergy exiled. But the English parliament's most specific condemnation was reserved for Richard Talbot who 'has notoriously assumed to himself the title of agent of the Roman Catholics of Ireland'. The king was asked that Talbot be 'dismissed out of all command, either civil or military, and forbidden any access to your majesty's court'. Charles, always a shrewd and politic monarch, knew that the time had come to change policy. The recent initiatives were abandoned and Talbot had to withdraw from court, returning for a while to Ireland and then going into exile abroad.

Nothing had been achieved: the position of Catholics in general and the land settlement in particular remained unchanged. Yet it is arguable that the early 1670s were crucial years for Richard Talbot, years when he began to develop a coherent strategy for the restoration of the Catholic gentry to their estates and to their former political and social role. Indeed a plan, apparently drafted around 1670 by his brother Peter, the recently appointed Catholic archbishop of Dublin, was found among his papers after he was forced out of London in 1673. This outlined ways in which the land settlement might be undone, the army put into reliable (i.e.

Catholic) hands, and Catholic judges appointed to the bench. These plans were a veritable blueprint for the policies he pursued in government some fifteen years later. By then, of course, with the accession of Talbot's patron, James duke of York, to the throne the opportunity for following a Catholic policy was never so promising.

With a Catholic king on the throne Talbot was acutely aware that no time was to be lost. James was fifty-two and his heir was his Protestant daughter Mary, wife of Prince William of Orange. *Persona grata* again at Whitehall, he set about exerting his considerable influence over James to achieve his long-term ambition, the restoration to the Catholic gentry of Ireland of the lands and status that had once been theirs.

James for his part was always ready to listen to his old friend and comrade-in-arms, whom he made earl of Tyrconnell soon after his accession. Furthermore, as a Catholic James believed that he had a particular duty to advance the interests of Catholics and Catholicism throughout his dominions. But that is not to say that he shared Tyrconnell's enthusiasm for a major modification of the land settlement or for restoring the Old English Catholic gentry to a political ascendancy they had lost long before they had been deprived of their estates. James was an English king who viewed his dominions from Whitehall. The interest of England might not be best served by taking the governance of Ireland, local as well as national, out of the hands of the Protestant gentry whose loyalty to the English connection, whatever about the monarchy, could never be in doubt. So in 1685 James started from the principle that everything should be done to ensure religious and civic freedom for his Catholic subjects in Ireland, but nothing must be done which might make Protestants fear for their estates and their security. It was Tyrconnell's task to talk the king out of this cautious stance.

Initially James kept his government in Dublin Castle in Protestant hands, which was temporarily reassuring for his Protestant subjects. It was not long, however, before some notable concessions were made to his Catholic subjects and it became clear that he was listening with increasing attention to the relentless advice of the newly ennobled Tyrconnell, who wisely spent most of his time at Whitehall to be close to the king's ear. He never missed an opportunity of reminding James that his best interest as king and his duty as a Catholic lay in helping his Catholic subjects in Ireland who had lost so much in the Cromwellian period and whose inclinations were more truly monarchical than the Protestant beneficiaries of the Cromwellian settlement.

Although Tyrconnell's appointment as lord deputy was not announced until the autumn of 1686 and he was not sworn in until the following February, his influence over policy became increasingly apparent during 1686. In June he travelled to Ireland to take command of the army, a humiliating snub for the sitting lord lieutenant, Lord Clarendon, who was thereby deprived of one of the traditional functions of a viceroy. As military commander Tyrconnell made it his business to purge the army of the 'disaffected', by which he meant Protestants, and to replace them with Catholic officers and soldiers, an undertaking which he carried out with efficiency and a considerable degree of success; by the end of the year the army in Ireland was predominantly Catholic.

1686 saw also the appointment of Catholic judges and the payment of Catholic bishops out of government funds. The Protestant and English viceroy had no choice but to acquiesce in these policies of which he profoundly disapproved, since his orders came directly from a Whitehall increasingly dominated by Tyrconnell so far as policy for Ireland was concerned. Whenever the king himself expressed doubts about the trend policy was taking, Tyrconnell used all the emotive rhetoric at his disposal to remind his monarch of the duty he owed to his hard-pressed but loyal Catholic subjects in Ireland.

By the time Tyrconnell was sworn in as lord deputy, in February 1687, it was clear that he was already the master of policy-making for Ireland. He could now press ahead with his policies and his strategic plan. More Catholic judges were appointed and more government money was made available to Catholic clergy (while Church of Ireland diocesan vacancies remained unfilled, suggesting that the Protestant Church was to become extinct through a process of natural wastage). The crucial development came in June 1687 when Tyrconnell, at his own instigation, was issued with a royal warrant empowering him to grant new charters to cities and corporate towns. The implications of this move went far beyond a reshaping of local government and a return to Catholic influence in the towns. It embraced the whole question of parliamentary representation: boroughs in Catholic hands would return Catholic members to a future Irish parliament and the overwhelmingly Catholic parliament which would be elected would seek to modify if not repeal the land settlement. In August he travelled to England for a meeting with the king at Chester and he returned to Ireland a few days later with his policies endorsed and his authority enhanced. He could now turn his attention to the principal preoccupation of his public life since the 1660s, the land question. By the following spring he was able to despatch two Catholic judges to London with elaborate proposals for a new land act.

Tyrconnell's policies were causing predictable and deepening anxiety in Protestant Ireland. With the army in Catholic hands, the land settlement under radical scrutiny and the absolute certainty that the next parliament would be overwhelmingly Catholic, many Protestants feared for the security of their lives and estates. However, it was not until well into 1688 that a Protestant exodus got under way. Many fled to England, fearing a repetition of the 1641 massacres, some settling on the west coast, others travelling to London and carrying with them stories of Catholic resurgence and arbitrary government. Their *bête noire* was Tyrconnell, the 'popish champion' as he was dubbed by protestant pamphleteers.

While the news from Ireland was seized upon in England by the king's critics for its propaganda value, it is difficult to estimate the degree of significance we should attach to Tyrconnell's policies in Ireland in bringing about the overthrow of James II's monarchy in the 'glorious revolution' of 1688. They certainly helped to heap coal on the king's head. Particularly outrageous in English eyes was Tyrconnell's Catholic army and if any one Irish consideration contributed significantly to the revolution, it was James's preparedness to rely upon a 'Popish' army from Ireland to uphold his authority in England. Nevertheless the 'glorious revolution' of 1688-9 was an essentially English *coup d'état* instigated by English politicians for essentially English reasons.

The overthrown of James II's monarchy in England and its replacement by the Protestant William and Mary of Orange, a process that lasted between November 1688 and February 1689, cast Tyrconnell's grand strategy for Ireland into total disarray. The Catholicization policies he had masterminded over the previous three years depended for their completion and durability on the Catholic James, so amenable to his advice, remaining in power in

Worsted in the Game

England for some years to come. With the king's support from Whitehall assured, Tyrconnell in Ireland was virtually unstoppable. With Whitehall in the hands of Protestant monarchs susceptible to the pleadings of the threatened Protestant proprietors of Ireland, the future prospects for his Catholic counter-revolution were distinctly unpromising. There could be no realistic possibility that the kingdom of Ireland could withstand the superior power of England and go its own way as a separate kingdom with a different monarchy.

The fateful news of James's flight to France and William's assertion of *de facto* power in England presented Tyrconnell with two possible courses of action. He could seek an accommodation with William, guaranteeing Catholics the position they had enjoyed at the end of Charles II's reign, or he could declare for the exiled James in the hope that the latter might in time regain his kingdom of England. For his part William, to the consternation of some Irish Protestant proprietors, was prepared to countenance an arrangement with Tyrconnell, but tentative contacts were aborted when Tyrconnell in late January 1689 decided to gamble on the second option and urged James to come to Ireland from his French exile. The deciding factor in Tyrconnell's decision was undoubtedly the promise of substantial French support for James's cause. This made it possible that the unfinished Catholic counter-revolution might yet be saved. James's presence in Ireland would offer an opportunity to salvage what Tyrconnell had come so close to achieving in the preceding three years, the restoration of the Catholic gentry to their estates and their political pre-eminence.

James was reluctant to travel to Ireland but did so in response to Tyrconnell's moral pressure (the king should 'consider whether you can with honour continue where you are when you may possess a kingdom of your own') and the virtual insistence of Louis XIV and the French government, who were anxious to open up a second front in the war against William or Orange. His arrival in Kinsale in March 1689 was followed by a triumphant progress to Dublin, where the flag over Dublin Castle bore the legend, 'Now or Never; Now and Forever'.

Re-united in Dublin, both James and Tyrconnell were agreed that the fundamental goal was James's restoration to his English throne. For James Ireland was a loyal and useful base from which to mount a military operation to take back his English and Scottish kingdoms. With this Tyrconnell had no argument since it was essential to have James back on his English throne to preserve the durability of any Irish settlement favourable to the Catholic gentry. But for Tyrconnell the opportunity was not to be lost of enacting that Catholic settlement into law while James was in Dublin. Here a clear difference over timing and priorities emerged between the king and his Catholic followers in Ireland. James was anxious not to alienate further his estranged English subjects with the legal overthrow of the Protestant land settlement in Ireland; Catholic claims could wait until his authority in England was re-established. But James's only certain supporters were Irish Catholics and it was on them that he relied for loyalty, military support and, most pressingly, that financial aid which would only be forthcoming if he summoned a parliament.

The 1689 parliament was overwhelming, though not exclusively Catholic, representative in large part of the Old English gentry (as a scrutiny of the members' surnames reveals). The Catholic composition of the House of Commons was quite predictable in the light of Tyrconnell's groundwork in putting the parliamentary boroughs back into Catholic hands in 1687 and 1688. Clearly a parliament so overwhelmingly Catholic would not be prepared to tolerate the continuance of a Protestant landed ascendancy established as recently as the 1650s. It passed with alacrity, and despite King James's reservations, an act repealing the Restoration land acts and another act attainting some 2,400 Protestant landowners, mentioned by name, finding them guilty of treason and therefore liable to forfeiture of their estates. With the passage of these statutes the Protestant ascendancy had been broken and the way was open for a return not just to the status quo of 1641 but to a situation where there would have been precious few Protestant landowners left in the country.

But the legislation of 1689 was soon a dead letter. The future of the Protestant ascendancy and of the Catholic gentry would not be determined in parliament but on the battlefield, and the victory of King William's forces at the Boyne in July of the following year decided the matter once and for all (though the war dragged on until 1691). Tyrconnell's determined and methodical seizure of power in the later 1680s, his attempt to reverse the course of recent history, was rendered null and void. Indeed if it had any long-term effect Tyrconnell's policies, together with the 1689 legislation, strengthened the resolve of the restored Protestant ascendancy to render any future attempts at a Catholic seizure of power utterly impossible, a determination which explains the passing of the penal laws in the 1690s and early 1700s, laws which further reduced the Catholic ownership of land and completed the depoliticization of the remaining Catholic gentry. But Tyrconnell himself never witnessed these events, dying quite suddenly in August 1691, just a few weeks before the war ended with the Treaty of Limerick. He had indeed come close to masterminding a remarkable counter-revolution. The survival of the revolution in landownership and politics of the mid-seventeenth century need not have been inevitable.

FURTHER READING

The standard and most authoritative work on this period is J.G. Simms, *Jacobite Ireland* (London 1969). Also by the same author are two Dublin Historical Association pamphlets: *The Jacobite Parliament of 1689* (Dundalk 1966) and *The Treaty of Limerick* (Dundalk 1961). Simms also provided an excellent narrative of events in Chapter xix of T.W. Moody, F.X. Martin and F.J. Byrne (eds), *A New History of Ireland* , vol. iii (Oxford 1976). John Miller's excellent biography, *James II. A Study in Kingship* (Hove 1978), contains a useful chapter on Ireland, while Miller's 'The earl of Tyrconnell and James II's Irish policy, 1685-1688' in *The Historical Journal*, xx (1977), pp. 802-23, provides a penetrating analysis of Tyrconnell's influence over the king. Some useful primary material is to be found in Philip W. Sergeant, *Little Jennings and Fighting Dick Talbot* (2 vols, London 1913), and Tyrconnell's letters to Queen Mary (of Modena) are in *Analecta Hibernica*, no. 4 (1932). There is a useful entry on Tyrconnell in the *Dictionary of National Biography* and a popular biography by Sir Charles Petrie, *The Great Tyrconnell* (Cork 1972).

Kane o Hara

Willm King Archbishop of Dublin 1702

obit. 1729. æt. 74.

Published Sep. 20.th 1803, by Wm Richardson York House, 31. Strand.

VII

ARCHBISHOP WILLIAM KING (1650-1729) and Colonial Nationalism

PATRICK KELLY

'I had rather suffer anything than betray my country ...'
King to Bishop Lindsay of Killaloe, 13 May 1698

*'No man ought to be silent when the liberty of our country
and the being of our parliament are at stake ...'*
King to Lord Percival, 25 January 1719/20

SENTIMENTS SUCH AS THESE might not immediately identify themselves as the utterances of an eighteenth-century Protestant bishop, yet their author William King, who lived from 1650 to 1729, was probably the most distinguished occupant of the see of Dublin since the Reformation. A brilliant scholar with a European reputation as a philosopher, he was also an able administrator, and an astute and influential politician, who won the respect of the polite world while maintaining a deep concern for the poor. Above all he was regarded as the champion of Irish independence against the incursions of the British ministry and parliament – 'to a ridiculous extravagance, national' as the exasperated lord lieutenant, the duke of Grafton, complained to Sir Robert Walpole in December 1723. Yet, despite the sincerity of his patriotism, the irony is that the passing of the British parliament's 1720 act declaring its full power and authority to make laws to bind the kingdom and people of Ireland was in large measure a direct consequence of King's actions.

From the age of Swift and the *Drapier's Letters* to that of Grattan and the achievement of parliamentary independence in 1782, the Sixth of George I, as the Declaratory Act was usually known, symbolized Ireland's subjection. It is this responsibility that sets William King, for all his brilliance and achievements, amongst the losers of Irish history. In what follows I wish to consider three main questions: what was it that William King and those who thought like him wished to achieve in regard to Irish independence? why did such aspirations come to be defeated? and how did the archbishop come to lead the settlers in this contest with the British ministry and parliament.

Though we generally think of Irish history since the Norman invasion in terms of the conflict between the English and the native Irish, relations between England and her settlers in Ireland have often been every bit as difficult. Indeed it was the need to control its own feudal dependents that first brought the English Crown directly into Irish affairs. In the seventeenth century the settlers came to see themselves as the beneficiaries of an independent Irish constitution regulating a kingdom possessed of its own parliament, courts and administrative structures, and owing allegiance to the sovereign in London as king or queen of Ireland. This 'dual monarchy' view of Anglo-Irish relations naturally appealed more to the English resident in Ireland than to those at home, and as the English parliament sought to take greater cognizance of its sovereign's doings, it concerned itself more and more with what went on in Ireland. During the Interregnum the parliamentary opponents of the Stuarts came to rule directly over Scotland and Ireland, and from 1653 to 1659 representatives of these kingdoms sat in the English parliament.

Although the Restoration in 1660 meant the re-establishment of an independent Irish parliament, no sessions were held between 1666 and the Revolution of 1688, and a considerable body of mostly economic legislation was enacted in England relating to Irish affairs. In the same period appeals from Ireland to the English House of Lords became necessary since there was no Irish House to which resort might be had. When after the Jacobite war sessions of the Irish parliament once more resumed, problems arose over both the question of the competence of the English parliament to legislate for Ireland and that of judicial appeals. Furthermore the post-Revolution settler community felt itself threatened by England in a way that had not been the case before the Catholic resurgence under James II. The vulnerability of the colony in the face of Catholic hostility had been exposed, together with the ambivalent attitude of Englishmen to those to their own race established in Ireland. The settlers also believed that England had failed to appreciate their losses and had endangered their future security by granting excessively favourable terms to the defeated Jacobites.

In the years that followed the Treaty of Limerick the aspirations of the settler community became increasingly clearly articulated and the question of legislative independence of the parliament in England achieved a central position in their thinking. They saw themselves as owing allegiance not to the English Crown in parliament but to an Irish sovereign resident in England who also happened to be the ruler of England and Scotland. The constitutional changes brought about by the 1688 Revolution in England made such an aspiration already an anachronism, but in the early 1690s while England was ruled by a Dutchman who fought against Louis XIV on the Continent, it still had a seeming reality. By the end of the century it had received two major blows; the first was the English act of 1699 prohibiting the export of woollen cloth from Ireland, while in 1700 an English Act of Resumption cancelled all grants made by King William of land forfeited during the Jacobite war. By then, however, the settlers' view of their position had produced a classic political work in William Molyneux's *The Case of Ireland's being bound by Acts of Parliament in England, stated* (1698), and had found an uncompromising advocate in the person of William King, then bishop of Derry.

Molyneux argued the case for legislative independence on two grounds. The first was the familiar one of precedent, that is from showing what Ireland's proper position had been in the past he sought to establish what her position should be in the present. The second was a new language for the assertion of Irish rights in terms of natural law, which claimed that 'Liberty seems the inherent Right of all Mankind' (*Case of Ireland*, ed. J. G. Simms, p. 24) and that to be bound by laws to the making of which one had not consented was the very condition of slavery. In recent years it has become usual to refer to the settler aspirations to independence, articulated in Molyneux's book, under the name 'colonial nationalism'. Criticism of the applicability of this term on the grounds that these rights were claimed exclusively on behalf of Protestants and that the essence of their case was the rejection of England's insistence on Ireland's colonial status does not seem particularly well founded. The aspiration to legislative independence was by no means confined to Protestants; when King James's largely Catholic parliament met in Dublin in 1689 it passed an act declaring the independence of Ireland from the English parliament. In the 1640s a similar claim had been advanced by the Catholic lawyer Patrick Darcy, and exactly the same position was taken in the only known body of Irish eighteenth-century Jacobite writing. Moreover, despite the assertions of both Catholics and Protestants that Ireland was an independent kingdom, what was at issue was essentially a colonial perception of relations with the mother country, a nationalism of strictly limited aspirations which involved no desire to break with England entirely.

King was not merely a spectator of the Anglo-Irish political dispute of the 1690s but was also directly involved at the forefront of the second area of conflict, namely the question of the ultimate resort of judicial appeals in Ireland. As bishop of Derry he had come into conflict over leases of land and fishery rights with the Irish Society, the London company which managed the Londonderry plantation. When the Irish House of Lords decided in King's favour, the Irish Society sought to reverse this by appealing to the House of Lords in England, who in 1698 ruled that the Irish body had no right to hear the particular appeal. King, whose main motive was to control the growth of Presbyterian influence in Derry, refused to accept this verdict and carried the other members of the Irish house with him in a prolonged though eventually fruitless resistance. Finally, a compromise was reached by private act of parliament in 1708.

However, the major principle as to the right of appeal from the Irish Lords to what following the Act of Union with Scotland in 1707 we must now call the British House of Lords was not settled. Two further cases in the early eighteenth century seemed to confirm the superior right of the British Lords at least in chancery cases, but the matter erupted in a violent and ultimately conclusive fashion with the Sherlock *versus* Annesley case in 1717. When James Annesley succeeded in obtaining an English verdict, the question arose of who in Ireland was responsible for implementing this decision and returning the disputed lands from Hesther Sherlock. Since the majority of Irish judges by this stage were appointees from England, it is not surprising that the barons of the Irish Exchequer were prepared to carry out the orders of the

British Lords and imprisoned the sheriff of Kildare for refusing to obey them.

When the Irish parliament reassembled in 1719, the House of Lords led by King were determined to reassert their position and in turn imprisoned the barons of the Exchequer. They also, again under King's direction, drew up a 'Representation' to King George in London asserting their traditional position and claiming that, in denying the ultimate judicial power of the Irish Lords, the British peers were attacking George's prerogative as king of Ireland. In the preamble the Irish Lords sketched out the theory of the Irish constitution as perceived by the settlers. In accordance with contemporary views that the form of government in a country was determined by an original contract, they claimed that the Irish constitution derived from the voluntary submission of the Irish princes to Henry II in 1172,' ... By (which) Agreement the People of Ireland obtained the Benefit of the English Laws, and many Privileges, particularly that of having a distinct Parliament, here as in England, and of having weighty and momentous matters relating to this Kingdom, treated of, discussed, and determined in the same' (*Journal of the House of Lords [Ireland]*, ii, p. 655). The actions of the Irish Lords and their attempt to spell out in their Representation their version of Anglo-Irish constitutional relations amounted to a direct challenge to their British counterparts, which the latter were not prepared to ignore.

As soon as the British parliament met, the Lords determined to enact legislation confirming their jurisdictional supremacy. At this point it seemed, however, happily for Ireland, that relations between Lords and Commons in the British parliament had been so soured by the abortive Peerage Bill in the previous session that the Commons would not back any measure increasing the authority of their rivals. An Irish lobby in London, many of whom sat in the British Commons, sought to exploit this hostility to Ireland's advantage. But the British ministry headed by Stanhope and Sunderland hit on the expedient of healing the breach between themselves and Robert Walpole, who had led the opposition to the peerage bill, by rallying Lords and Commons around a bill which would increase the powers of the British parliament as a whole in asserting the legislative as well as the jurisdictional subordination of the Irish parliament. The result was a triumph for the ministry and the passing of 'An Act for the better securing the Dependency of the Kingdom of Ireland upon the Crown of Great Britain', usually known as the Declaratory Act, or Sixth of George I. A bonus for Stanhope was the chance to revenge himself on the Church of Ireland lobby led by King which in 1719 had thrown out his bill for toleration of Protestant dissenters in Ireland. But whatever the motives of the ministry, the aspirations of the colonists in Ireland since 1691 to an independent kingdom with its own sovereign parliament had received a setback, which was not to be reversed till the pressures of the American war forced the second Rockingham ministry to restore parliamentary independence in 1782. What concerns us now, however, is not the future development of colonial nationalism but why Archbishop King should have been its champion in the late seventeenth and early eighteenth centuries.

The basis of King's prestige amongst the settler community rested on a combination of his courageous behaviour during the Jacobite regime in 1689-90 and his authorship of *The State of the Protestants in Ireland, under the late King James's Government* (1691). The latter was the most influential justification of the Irish Protestants' repudiation of allegiance to James II, on the basis of the natural right to liberty and self-preservation. By birth and origin William King was an unlikely starter as a spokesman for the Anglican ascendancy in Ireland. His father had been a Scotsman who, rather than accept the Solemn League and Covenant against Charles I, had abandoned his farmstead and come to Ireland, settling in Antrim sometime in the 1640s. The blight of civil war and its accompanying destruction lay heavy over King's childhood, as we learn from the Latin autobiography which he wrote in 1702. Despite his father's practice of household prayers and Bible reading, King claimed that he and his school-fellows had never been taught to pray and that not till he came to Trinity at seventeen did anyone impart to him a sense of personal religion. Even allowing for his later position as a convert to Anglicanism, readers of the autobiography cannot but directly feel the bleakness of the war-torn Ulster of King's childhood and appreciate the intensity of his conviction of the divine mercy that had rescued him from such a condition. Though Trinity provided King with his opportunity, his College years were a time of unrelenting study and poverty. In the end he failed to obtain the College fellowship for which he had hoped, but sufficiently distinguished himself to win the patronage of Archbishop Parker of Tuam. Parker first saved King from disappearing to the obscurity of a country parish, and on his own transfer to Dublin brought him to the important parish of St Werburgh's. Here King's interest in intellectual life once more reawakened, together with a new concern for public affairs.

King's role as a leader of Protestant opinion began in earnest during the Catholic resurgence under James II. By the time the Revolution occurred in England and James fled to safety in France, King had been elected dean of St Patrick's and, following the withdrawal of Archbishop Marsh, found himself in charge of the Dublin diocese. With the arrival of James II in Dublin in March 1689 King, together with his friend Anthony Dopping, bishop of Meath, was the recognized leader of the Protestant community. On two occasions he found himself imprisoned as a danger to the Jacobites; and this experience of threat and prison accomplished what James and Tyrconnell's earlier treatment of the Protestants had failed to do, namely brought King to repudiate the teaching of passive obedience to the monarch, which he had imbued from his Anglican teachers. Although in strict moral terms King might perhaps be said to have hallowed a pragmatism akin to that of those who had earlier fled to join William in England, King could well argue that he had not abandoned James, till James had first abandoned him.

What happened during the Jacobite war powerfully reinforced King's earlier sense that he had been singled out by Providence to fulfil a particular role in the Church and lay state. The God who had delivered him from the darkness of unregenerate Presbyterianism to serve in the true Church had once more saved him, together with the Protestant people of Ireland. This view comes out very strongly both in the diary which King kept in 1689-90 and in the thanksgiving sermon which he preached before William of Orange following the restoration of Dublin to Protestant control. King was left with an overwhelming conviction that the Church of Ireland and the traditional secular constitution represented the sole bulwark against disorder of the kind that had so balefully overshadowed his childhood and more recently threatened the destruction of his co-religionists. The view that the establishment in Church and state constituted the sole bulwark against the renewal of anarchy was not uncommon in Restoration England, and though we do not know how widespread such feelings were amongst Irish Protestants after the

Jacobite war, we may hazard a guess from the popularity of King's *State of the Protestants* that they exercised a not inconsiderable appeal. In King's case it is essential to appreciate the strength of his conviction of both the providential role of the Protestant settler community and the unique status of the constitution in Church and state as the bulwark against anarchy. It is this conviction above all else that provides the key to a political philosophy which on a superficial reading may seem the acme of self-interested banality – particularly when set in conjunction with his well-known *Essay on the Origin of Evil* (1702).

This concept of the sacrosanctity of the constitution comes out very clearly in King's reflections on the consequences of the 1720 Declaratory Act, which he stigmatized as the demise of the independent Irish constitution. He saw the constitution as the guarantee of the liberties and privileges of the subject, and argued that the nation's happiness and prosperity depended on readiness to defend it, if need be, by force. This equation had remained the basis of King's thinking from *The State of the Protestants* in 1691. The dangers of submission to illegal authority seemed to him almost as threatening in 1720 as under James II, and he lamented that he lacked the energy to put the case for liberty which was as necessary now as then.

King's perception of the threat imposed by political dependence was by no means restricted to abstract issues. He saw a very real connection between political independence for an Irish parliament and economic prosperity. Though this theme also surfaced briefly in *The State of the Protestants*, it came out most clearly in his reaction to the English parliament's threat to destroy Irish woollen manufacture in 1698. Indeed King actually prepared for publication at this stage a short pamphlet in which he anticipated many of the political arguments of Molyneux's *Case of Ireland Stated*, and dealt at much greater length with the economic issues. In the 1720s King, like Swift, feared that Ireland's money supply and economy would be at the mercy of those in the British ministry and parliament who had already shown that they regarded Ireland as fit for exploitation. For this reason he opposed the 1720-1 Bank project and in 1723-5 led the successful opposition to Wood's Halfpence, hoping that in the long run the preponderance of force over constitutional right would not be allowed to prevail. As he wrote at the height of the Sherlock *versus* Annesly controversy:

Whatever the consequence I think it fit to put it to an issue, that we may not be in the present uncertainty and dissension, and our claim will remain upon record, and though overborn at present ... it may serve us instead when more favourable circumstances happen. (King to Lord Southwell, 8 January 1719/20)

Such a comment is also interesting in bringing out the difference between the nature of King's optimistic patriotism and that of Swift, as instanced in the latter's famous comment on Ireland's dependent status: '... in Reason, all Government without the Consent of the Governed, is the very Definition of Slavery; But in fact, Eleven Men well armed, will certainly subdue one single Man in his shirt' (*Fourth Drapier's Letter*, 1724).

When we consider the circumstances in which legislative independence was regained in 1782, it is hard to determine whether the archbishop or his dean was the better political prophet.

FURTHER READING

The standard life of William King is *A Great Archbishop of Dublin: William King D.D. 1650-1729*, ed. C. S. King, (Dublin 1906), which contains his Autobiography of 1702 and many extracts from his letters and papers. Other extracts from his letters are found in Irvin Ehrenpreis, *Swift: the Man, his Works, and the Age*, (3 vols. London: 1962; Cambridge Mass. 1967, 1983), which is also valuable for the background. On the general history of the period, see F. G. James, *Ireland and the Empire, 1691-1770* (Princeton 1973); David Dickson, *New Foundations: Ireland, 1660-1800* (Dublin 1987), and *A New History of Ireland*, vol. iv, 'Eighteenth-Century Ireland, 1691-1800', eds. T. W. Moody and W. E. Vaughan, (Oxford 1986). Also useful are J. G. Simms, *William Molyneux of Dublin, 1656-1698,* ed. P. H. Kelly (Dublin 1982); Caroline Robbins, *The Eighteenth-Century Commonwealthman* (Cambridge, Mass. 1959), and Louis Landa, *Swift and the Church of Ireland* (Oxford 1954). On colonial nationalism, see J. G. Simms, *Colonial Nationalism, 1698-1776* (Cork 1976), and D. G. Boyce, *Nationalism in Ireland* (Dublin 1982), pp. 102-8. The important new interpretation of the background to the

1720 Declaratory Act comes from Isolde Victory, 'Colonial Nationalism in Ireland, 1691-1725' (unpublished Ph.D. thesis, Trinity College, Dublin 1985). For further recent work on King's political role and opinions, see Andrew Carpenter, 'William King and the Threats to the Church of Ireland during the Reign of James II', *Irish Historical Studies*, xviii (1972), pp. 22-7, and David Berman, 'The Jacobitism of Berkeley's Passive Obedience', *Journal of the History of Ideas*, vol. xlvii (1986), pp. 309-19.

Among William King's own writings the most important for present purposes are *The State of the Protestants in Ireland, under the late King James's Government (1691)*, and his views on the 1698 Irish woollens crisis published in Patrick Kelly, 'A Pamphlet Attributed to John Toland and an Unpublished Reply by Archbishop William King' in *Topoi*, vol. iv (1985), pp. 81-90. His prison diary for 1689 has been edited by H. J. Lawlor as *The Diary of William King ... during his imprisonment in Dublin Castle 1689* (Dublin 1903). King's general philosophical position is brought out in *An Essay on the Origin of Evil*, ed. and trans. W. Warburton 1731 (New York 1978), and *A Sermon on Predestination*, ed. D. Berman, (Dublin 1976). King's letterbooks in Trinity College, Dublin, MS 750, are the source for his political opinion in 1698 and 1719-20. See also, William Molyneux, *The Case of Ireland's being bound by Acts of Parliament in England, stated*, ed. J. G. Simms (Dublin 1977).

J.W.Allais Lithog

VIII

HENRY FLOOD (1732-91)
and the Eighteenth-Century Irish Patriots

DAVID DICKSON

ONE OF THE MORE SENSATIONAL duels of eighteenth-century
Ireland was fought outside Kilkenny city in September 1769
between two prominent Protestant landowners, James Agar MP
and Henry Flood MP. The immediate background is obscure, but
the challenge from Agar was the second he had issued that year,
and was the culmination of a bitter feud between the Flood and
Agar families for control of the corporation of Callan and, by
extension, for control over who represented Callan in the Irish
parliament. Most duels between gentlemen did not have fatal
consequences, but on this occasion the fifty-six year old Agar was
shot dead by Flood, twenty years his junior. Flood underwent trial
for murder in the following year but was honourably discharged.
Yet the Agar/Flood struggle for Callan borough continued for
more than a decade, with the Flood party gradually reduced to
electoral impotence.

Henry Flood's claim to greatness does not rest on such events.
Yet it was typical of so much in Flood's life: theatrical
confrontations, tactical victories, strategic defeat. Flood's public
career in Ireland was contained within the quarter-century
between George III's accession in 1760 and the temporary
stabilization of Irish politics in 1785; during that time he was
always one of the key parliamentary actors, on occasion the most
independent figure in Irish politics.

In all popular accounts of this period, when the constitutional
status of the Irish parliament *vis-à-vis* Westminster was
transformed, Flood is juxtaposed with his junior, Henry Grattan,
and the poisonous rivalry between them underlined: Grattan the
emotional radical, hero of April 1782 and midwife of the new

parliamentary constitution, whose political career and reputation survived another forty years; and Flood the darker and more elusive figure, more logical in his powers of analysis, intellectually more gifted, personally more arrogant and repeatedly frustrated in his aspirations, wrong-footed at key moments (not least in April 1782), and all but forgotten by the time of the Union. Grattan's remains lie in Westminster Abbey, Flood's lie hidden in Burnchurch graveyard, County Kilkenny. Grattan has had many biographers, Flood none. The large-scale destruction of Flood's personal papers shortly after his death partly explains this, but his omission from the pantheon of Irish heroes that was constructed by nationalist writers in the nineteenth century was for more substantial reasons: his appeal to later generations was much less than Grattan's because of the restricted definition of his 'patriotism' – to use a term that had no nationalist connotations when attached to Flood in the 1760s, but had exclusively nationalist connotations by the later nineteenth century.

What of the background of this politician whom John Philpot Curran later labelled 'unmeasurably the greatest man of his time in Ireland' (*Dict. Nat. Biog.* vii, p. 334)? Flood's paternal grandfather, a Williamite soldier, had married Anne Warden, a Kilkenny heiress, and four of the eight sons of the marriage established themselves as county gentry on fragments of the dismembered Ormond estate south of Kilkenny city. The eldest son, Warden Flood, trained for the law and went to the top of his profession to become Lord Chief Justice in 1760, an achievement that reflected the political friendship and influence of the strongest Co. Kilkenny political dynasty, the Ponsonbys. By the mid-eighteenth century this family had become one of the three leading political mafias in Ireland, power-brokers in parliament – or 'undertakers' as they were then called – whose strength lay in their skills in managing the House of Commons for the government, and in extracting political patronage in return.

Henry Flood was the elder son of the Lord Chief Justice; he was born in 1732 shortly before his parents actually married. Like Grattan, Foster, Fitzgibbon and many of the other notables of late eighteenth-century Irish politics, Flood grew up in a wealthy Dublin legal household. He was a contemporary of Edmund Burke at TCD, and went on to complete his university education at Oxford and his legal training in London. He never practised at the bar, indeed spent most his 'twenties in England moving in literary, theatrical and artistic circles, befriending other peripatetic Anglo-Irishmen including the young Lord Charlemont. He returned to Ireland in 1759 when one of the parliamentary seats for County Kilkenny fell vacant, courtesy of the Ponsonbys. However, on the dissolution of parliament a year later, the Ponsonbys were less accommodating and at first Flood failed to secure even his father's old seat at Callan in the 1761 general election. However, after a parliamentary enquiry, he triumphed over James Agar and re-entered the House of Commons.

Flood's reputation as an outstanding parliamentary speaker and opposition politician was built on his performances during the 1760s. At this time a succession of uninspiring viceroys, political flux in London, and the natural demise of several of the old undertakers provided scope for those MPs who wished to challenge the power of the Irish government – and, by extension, the ministry in London – in parliamentary affairs.

Nearly all the 300 MPs elected in 1761 were Protestant landed gentlemen or lawyers with landed connections. The majority were either associated with one of the great undertaker families or were government office-holders, place-men, or otherwise dependent on Castle favour. A substantial minority were unconnected independents, but most of these were open to government blandishments; a small rump stayed in opposition on principle. The latter element, few in number but highly articulate, freely borrowed the language and sentiments of the equivalent independent group in the Westminster parliament; indeed the tag 'patriot' was itself borrowed from England. The Irish 'Patriots' were a motley group – lawyers, middle-ranking country gentry, a few young aristocrats like the earl of Charlemont, and a former Dublin apothecary, the radical Charles Lucas. Ideologically they were heirs of the 'country' Whigs in England, but there was no agreed patriot programme, each activist having a slightly different set of legislative priorities. They were however united in seeking to curb the power of the Irish executive within parliament, to strengthen the legislative and watch-dog role of the House of Commons, to increase the independence of the judiciary from 'Crown' influence, and to reduce government expenditure. One policy had already been widely canvassed in the 1761 election, that of limiting the duration of parliament to seven years (as opposed to the current limit of the lifetime of the monarch). It was taken as axiomatic that regular general elections would make MPs more responsive to the electorate and less easily controlled, whether by Dublin Castle or by the undertakers. In session after session during the 1760s Flood and Lucas introduced bills to limit the life of the parliament and they actually received the backing of a majority of MPs, many of whom realized that their ostensible support for a popular cause would cost them nothing; they assumed that such daring legislation would always be vetoed at the Irish or the British Privy Councils. Most MPs, certainly the undertakers, were happy to work within the existing scheme of things, tolerating the restricted legislative powers of the Irish parliament and the superior role of the two Priory Councils, but there had always been a handful who had protested at the unconstitutionality of this. Flood became the best informed critic of the official justification for Ireland's dependent constitutional status; he made repeated and telling attacks on the way the fifteenth-century Poynings' law was now being interpreted and enforced.

Flood's carefully constructed oratory, on this and other issues, was shaped by his deep classical education and his interest in the theatre. It won him national celebrity as he triumphed over government supporters in debate. The Castle came to respect him as an opponent. And yet he was not a political outsider like Lucas. He was still cautiously friendly with the Flood family's old Kilkenny allies, the Ponsonbys – now at the zenith of their power – and his marriage to a wealthy Beresford bride in 1762 created the possibility of a political alliance with one of the second-rank parliamentary factions. Indeed as early as 1766 Flood's political ambitions were rising: he toyed with the idea of securing an English parliamentary seat and of following Edmund Burke on a more rewarding political career at the imperial centre. He also seems to have privately offered to give political support to an Irish government led by the earl of Bristol in 1767 – even to take office in it – if certain patriot measures were adopted, in particular if Poynings' law was modified. Bristol, however, was only viceroy for a few months and never reached Ireland before his recall.

His successor, Viscount Townshend, was the first strong and centralizing chief governor in Dublin Castle for decades. Townshend was determined to push through the highly unpopular proposal that the Irish financial contribution to the imperial army should be raised by a third, and he played off the different political factions within the Dublin parliament, weakened the old undertakers, and raised more pliable new ones, notably the Beresfords, to power. But Townshend's first stroke was to accede to the patriot demand for finite parliaments and regular general elections.

In the first such general election held in 1768 Flood was proposed as one of the candidates for the genuinely 'open' constituency of Dublin City, many of whose 4000 freemen were avid readers of the new opposition press which had consistently backed the patriots. For reasons unknown, Flood turned down the chance to run with Lucas in the capital, and stood for County Kilkenny in alliance with Edmund Butler, against James Agar's nephew and Speaker Ponsonby. But as he later observed, 'this county ... is not the soil of patriotism' (W. Flood, *Memoirs*, p. 347), and he was soundly defeated, coming fourth behind his young Butler ally. However, helped by the strong-arm tactics of his relatives, Flood continued to hold the upper hand in Callan: Henry and his cousin John were returned for the borough. Even by the standards of eighteenth-century electoral malpractice, the violence and disorder surrounding municipal and parliamentary elections at Callan were unusual. Patriot ideology was of little relevance in determining how the heavily bribed freemen and burgesses would vote. The number of such voters was quite large for a modest market town with few Protestants – probably in excess of a hundred – but many were non-resident. Only the financial muscle of the Flood clan and their stated willingness to go 'knee deep in blood for Callan' (P.R.O.I. Prim MS 37) had secured electoral victory. The Agars, who had up until then managed to hold on to one of the Callan seats, were furious and smouldering resentments among the south Kilkenny gentry several generations old were inflamed by the electoral competition. The fatal duel a year later was the *coup de grâce*.

Flood's local excitements did not stop him from being at the centre of the parliamentary conflict with Townshend. The patriot tail wagged the opposition dog, with Flood and Charlemont planning a grand alliance linking the threatened undertakers and the patriot MPs against Townshend's government and 'the arbitrary dictation of an English administration' (Bartlett, 'Opposition', p. 326). Among the flurry of pamphlet publications during 1769 and 1770, an edition of William Molyneux's classic defence of the independence of the Irish parliament, *The Case of Ireland's being bound by Acts of Parliament in England*, stated, first published in 1698, appeared; it contained a powerful new introductory essay, and Flood was rumoured to be the author.

The opposition challenge to the strong viceroy crumbled. In due course Townshend broke the Ponsonbys, tamed other undertakers, and built up a party loyal to the Castle in the Commons. In the face of this, Flood changed his tactics but retained his personal ambitions. His critics in the 1770s believed that he was becoming as greedy for office and power as any MP, merely operating behind 'the mask of patriotism' (Bodkin, 'Irish Parliament, 1773', p. 197), whereas he protested that he was only interested in securing certain political objectives, all broadly tending to strengthen the constitutional status of the Irish parliament. The truth must lie somewhere in between: his popularity in the sixties, his good political contacts in London and his intellectual athleticism together gave him a very high sense of his own importance, which many found off-putting. It was difficult being the brightest goldfish in a small tank when there was a larger, more alluring pond nearby.

After Townshend's five-year administration came that of the more subtle and relaxed Lord Harcourt. Parliament was gradually brought – or rather bought – over, and Irish politics were remarkably calm as the storm clouds gathered over colonial America. Flood engaged in an elaborate three-year courtship with Harcourt, and was finally given the vice-treasurership of Ireland in 1775, an office with no executive function but which raised his personal income by a half. To Flood's old friend Charlemont, this was almost a betrayal: office was potentially corrupting and office in a government that supported the suppression of American liberties was even more offensive. Flood of course saw it differently. Harcourt's administration had undone some of Townshend's financial policies which Flood had opposed, and Harcourt had supported the patriot policy of a tax on absentee rents: Flood seems to have convinced himself that it was a well-meaning regime. However, the real reason for Flood's acceptance of government office was the frustration at the way his career was unfolding: leadership of a fragmented patriot opposition was a barren occupation for one who sought access to power and influence.

It was a bad decision for Flood. Harcourt was succeeded in 1776 by perhaps the weakest government in eighteenth-century Ireland; it was headed by the earl of Buckinghamshire, who remained at the Castle for most of the American war. Flood was shackled to a government which gradually lost the initiative in the Irish House of Commons, tottered on the the verge of exchequer bankruptcy in 1778, and had to give ground to a reborn and more broadly based patriotic opposition in 1779 and 1780. And, despite being a member of the Irish Privy Council, he failed to influence or modify government policy; he remained an almost silent member of government until his loyalty began to waver visibly in 1779. Younger men, notably Henry Grattan and Barry Yelverton, had taken his place as the articulate leaders of anti-government sentiment in the Irish parliament. And at the *local* level things went wrong for Flood too. He was defeated again in the County Kilkenny election of 1776, and although he was returned for Callan, the result was challenged in parliament; George Agar, the duellist's son, was given the seat in his place. Such a parliamentary decision reflected both Flood's new weakness in the Commons, and the failure of government to support his cause. As it turned out, Callan was now lost forever, and Flood was forced to purchase seats from friendly borough owners, in 1777 and again in 1783. Kilkenny had rejected Flood – a measure of the greater guile of the Agars and their allies than of the political opinions of local Protestant voters.

But Flood's moment of triumph was yet to be. His first display of independence from the administration came late in 1779, during the extra-parliamentary agitation for commercial equality between Ireland and Britain in foreign and colonial trade – 'free trade' as Flood had called it, and all echoed him. Abolition of these commercial restrictions had long been part of the agenda of opposition MPs – although it was not one of the issues which Flood had personally campaigned for. But he jumped on the opposition band-wagon and was willing to be identified with the newly politicized Volunteer corps. These locally organized unofficial militias were completely dominated by the landed gentry, and their military threat to the government was mere bluff, but they were successfully used from 1779 to intimidate a weak administration. Flood was involved in Dublin and Kilkenny corps.

With free trade reluctantly granted by London in December 1779, pressure for reform of the constitutional status of the Irish parliament built up again, and on this Flood could not stand back. In 1781 he entered the race with the younger politicians to extract a new round of concessions. The American war was by now all but lost and the English ministry of Lord North was nearing its end; Flood distanced himself irrevocably from the Castle, and later that year he was removed from the Council and the Vice-Treasurership. He had been strangely slow to make the final move. To his chagrin, Grattan and Yelverton remained the rhetorical – if not the actual – leaders of the opposition groundswell which in April 1782 culminated in the repeal of Poynings' Law and the removal from the British statute book of Westminster's offensive claim (in the Declaratory Act of 1720) to legislate for Ireland.

The opportunist in Flood and his legal instincts gave him the chance to trump Grattan some months later and to re-establish his credentials as patriot leader. With only a handful of MPs in support he challenged Grattan's acceptance of the April concordat with London: simple repeal of the Declaratory Act was meaningless, he argued; a formal renunciation by Westminster of its superior status *vis-à-vis* Dublin was required. Flood managed to divide Protestant opinion across the country on the issue and he was fortuitously helped by unwise and provocative statements in London about the imperial relationship and Ireland's unresolved position. The suspicions of the naturally suspicious were roused. Flood succeeded – after months of local campaigning – in frightening the government, and a renunciation act of sorts was passed at Westminster early in 1783. Yet he signally failed to capitalize on his undoubted personal popularity around the country in the Irish general election later that year; he had always said he was averse to building up parliamentary alliances or dependents on principle, and the politics of the claret bottle were never his *forte*.

During the election a new issue emerged: parliamentary reform. The call for this measure was surfacing after four years of unprecedented political activity both in Dublin and in many Irish counties; non-landowning voters had now become more aware of the great issues of the day, thanks to the political activities of the dozens of Volunteer corps and the extension of the provincial press. In England a novel agitation for parliamentary reform had developed slightly earlier in the course of the American war. 'Reform' in this context meant shorter parliaments, a reduction in the relative weight and importance of the small borough seats (which the great landed families and government placemen seemed to monopolize) and a corresponding strengthening of county representation. Many of those who had first espoused reform, both in England and in Ireland, were in fact ambitious landowners who wished to enhance their local popularity, if possible at the expense of landowners who already controlled boroughs. The leading Irish reformers used the network of volunteer corps during 1783 to give the reform campaign country-wide momentum.

Flood supported but did not direct this movement. Like many other MPs, he depended at that stage on the constituency *status quo*, the market in 'closed' or pocket parliamentary seats, to get into parliament. But his resentment at the family's tribulations in Kilkenny reinforced his intellectual disposition towards a policy that would strengthen, as he saw it, the independence of the Irish parliament.

A national convention made up of 186 representatives of most of the local Volunteer corps met at the Rotunda Assembly Rooms in Dublin in November 1783. It included 59 MPs, half a dozen peers and a few Catholic Volunteers – all landed gentry. Yet it was seen by most in the freshly elected House of Commons a quarter of a mile away as a dangerous threat to the dignity of parliament itself. The Irish government, by fairly astute stage management, managed to drive a wedge between the two assemblies. The Convention's intended function was to draft a general plan of parliamentary reform, and to present it to the Commons. The conflicting motives and incoherent aims of the reformers were quite apparent in the early days of its deliberations. Flood, there as a Volunteer delegate, was co-opted on to the drafting committee, and his political experience immediately made itself felt. He knocked heads together and devised what was a fairly moderate reform plan – three-year parliaments, a wider county franchise, the re-drawing of borough boundaries, a bribery oath for MPs, and the streamlining of election procedures. It reflected Flood's hard-learnt local lessons. Wearing his Volunteer uniform, he brought this plan to the Commons' chamber and solemnly presented it; it was thrown out by a vote of more than 2 to 1 against. Government supporters and borough MPs were nearly all opposed to it. County MPs – who had now to be more sensitive of 'public opinion' – for the most part backed Flood. Deterred somewhat but not beaten, the reform movement continued. After a winter of petition-gathering and county-freeholder meetings,

Flood introduced the bill into the Commons again the next spring. It was rejected by a similar margin.

Flood was too old a politician to be surprised. Indeed other reformers were doubtful of his total commitment to the reform movement; William Drennan, the rising star of Presbyterian radicalism, was certainly unimpressed: 'Times of reformation require impetuosity of spirit. Our religious reformation required such a man as Luther. Flood is too wise, too cool, perhaps too selfish to be a Luther in civil reform' (Drennan to Bruce, Dec. 1783, P.R.O.N.I. D553/17). The charge of selfishness is hard to deny. Once again Flood was turning his eyes to Westminster politics – and at last he managed to purchase an English parliamentary seat. His decision to transfer to London at this stage of his life, when he was past fifty, is nevertheless puzzling. He seemed unwilling to exploit the fact that he was leader of the radical wing of the Irish patriots, within and outside parliament. There was certainly no financial motive: with a growing rental and twenty children to provide for, he was remarkably unencumbered. There are two possible answers: he may have hoped for great things at Westminster with the ministerial changes during 1783, notably the meteoric rise of William Pitt the younger. Or he may have sought a retreat from his new role as leader of the more radical patriots because his views on the place of Catholics in a reformed political system did not coincide with the majority of advanced radicals in east Ulster and Dublin. He prided himself on his consistency: 'We should allow [Roman Catholics] ... to purchase lands, but we should carefully guard against their possessing any power in the state' (*Parliamentary Register ... Ireland*, i, p.253), by which he meant the vote and the right to membership of corporations and parliament. The question of the Catholic right to vote divided Irish parliamentary reformers down the middle, although the issue had been temporarily fudged at the Rotunda reform convention.

Flood played little further part in Irish politics, rarely attending parliament after 1784. He sat somewhat more regularly at Westminster until 1790, speaking occasionally and sometimes with the impact he had had in Dublin. But he was a lone voice, lacking close political friends in the house, and no doors opened for him. In the flurry for seats in the 1790 elections, he failed to get one in either Westminster or in College Green. He died after a short illness next year, aged fifty-nine, just as he was completing the reconstruction of Farmley, his small County Kilkenny mansion.

Flood's career points to two general observations about eighteenth-century Ireland. First, Flood was quintessentially a parliament man; like most of the gentry he saw the Irish parliament, for all its faults, as the key to control over the destinies of his class and of his country. The exercise of political power *outside* parliament, the structure of the Irish government, and the relationship between political power and economic power were for him all derivative issues. This legalistic obsession with parliament diverted the patriots – and most of the radicals after them – from probing more fundamental aspects of political reform.

Secondly, there is the ambiguity in the terms of references of Flood's patriotism: on the face of it, the Catholic majority were irrevocably damned by past association with arbitrary government and were not fit members of the political nation – a view shared by most of Flood's friends in the 1760s. By the 1780s some entertained the possibility of widening the political nation and of accepting propertied Catholics as equally committed to the defence of the liberties of the subject. Yet even for those like Flood who still rejected this possibility, there was a new view of the country and its past in the air. In Flood's case this was only revealed in his will: he left his patrimonial estate, on the death of his widow, to Trinity College for the establishment of a professorship in Irish, and for the purchase of Irish manuscripts. This bequest – the equivalent of more than £10 million in late twentieth-century values – would have given a dramatic impetus to the nineteenth-century reconstruction of the Gaelic past. Flood never enlarged on his motives. All we know is that he was a founder member of the Royal Irish Academy in 1785, and to his death he remained a close friend of Charlemont, Vallencey and other aristocratic antiquarians; none of them rivalled him in directing such patronage towards Gaelic scholarship. But here again Flood was to be a loser: his cousin challenged the will in the courts (on the grounds of Flood's illegitimacy) and Trinity never received Flood's remarkable bequest.

FURTHER READING

The destruction of most of Flood's personal papers after his death is only partly compensated for by the survival of his private communications in the collections of other eighteenth-century Irish politicians. The most important such collection are the Rosse Papers at Birr Castle. Two interesting but limited selections of letters and papers relating to his political career were published by relatives in the early nineteenth century: [Thomas Flood] (ed.) *Original letters ... to the Rt Hon. Henry Flood* (London 1820), and Warden Flood (ed.), *Memoirs of the Life and Correspondence of the Rt Hon. Henry Flood* (Dublin 1838); the latter includes a not entirely uncritical biographical essay by the editor.

Since the early nineteenth century, Lecky's essay on Flood (in *The Leaders of Public Opinion in Ireland* [London 1871]), and G.F.R Barker's entry on Flood in the *Dictionary of National Biography* are the only attempts at summarizing and assessing his career. In R.B.McDowell's writings on eighteenth-century Irish politics, notably his *Irish Public Opinion 1750-1800* (London 1944) and his *Ireland in the Age of Imperialism and Revolution* (Oxford 1979), Flood's parliamentary and intellectual milieu is sketched out admirably. Also of value are M. Bodkin, 'Notes on the Irish Parliament in 1773', *Proc. R.I.A.*, xlviii, C (1942); Theresa O'Connor, 'The Conflict between Flood and Grattan, 1782-3' in H.A. Cronne, T.W.Moody and D.B.Quinn (eds), *Essays in British History ...* (London 1949); [Mary Drummond] entry on 'Henry Flood', in Sir Lewis Namier and John Brooke (eds), *The House of Commons, 1754-1790* (London 1964), ii, pp. 441-2; Thomas Bartlett, 'Opposition in late Eighteenth-Century Ireland: the Case of the Townshend Viceroyalty', *Ir. Hist. Stud.*, xxii, 88 (Sept. 1981), pp. 313-30; and J. Th. Leersen, *Mere Irish and Fior-Ghael: Studies in the Idea of Irish Nationality ...* (Amsterdam 1986), pp. 420-1. A full-length biography of Flood remains a necessary if daunting item on the agenda of eighteenth-century Irish historians.

Worsted in the Game

James F. Tate

IX

JAMES FINTAN LALOR (1807-49)
and Rural Revolution

MARY E. DALY

WHETHER JAMES FINTAN LALOR fully merits the status of 'loser' in Irish history is a matter of some debate. In terms of his own lifetime the matter is unequivocal. At his death Lalor had been involved in a long series of failures, from his letter to British Prime Minister Sir Robert Peel in 1843 when he attempted to induce new thinking on the Irish question, his failure to be chosen among the leaders of the 1848 rebellion and his final involvement in a shambles of a rebellion in Tipperary in 1849. But can somebody who inspired the New Departure and Land League of 1879, who was numbered by Pearse among the four evangelists of Irish nationalism and whose words supplied the motto for James Connolly's Irish Citizen Army be truly regarded as a failure? Success or failure, Lalor's story is interesting because it charts a personal journey from romantic reform to full-blown revolution, and shows the reaction of one Irishman to the trauma of the Great Famine.

James Fintan Lalor was born in 1807, the eldest son of Patrick Lalor of Tenakill, County Laois. His father is generally described as a 'gentleman farmer', he would more accurately be called a farmer-cum-middleman who controlled approximately a thousand acres of good farming land, some he sublet, the remainder he farmed himself. The family belonged to the ranks of the upwardly mobile Catholic middle classes, a background not dissimilar to that of Daniel O'Connell or Cardinal Paul Cullen. It was a politically minded household. Patrick Lalor was a supporter of O'Connell who sprang to public notice when he became leader as a result of the anti-tithe movement in County Laois. In 1833 he became an O'Connellite, or Liberal MP and though he lost his seat in 1835, he remained active in politics, serving as a Poor Law Guardian for the Mountmellick Union.

James Fintan Lalor his eldest son, was a hunchback who suffered from poor health through his life. As a result most of his schooling took place at home, though he spent one year at Carlow College and while legend suggests that he was briefly apprenticed to a local doctor or apothecary, he also appears to have spent most of his adult life in this father's house. He became interested in the temperance movement, a cause led by Father Mathew, which was sweeping Ireland in the late thirties and early forties, and from the nucleus of his local temperance group he set up the Shamrock Friendly Society, a group which, among other activities, aimed at 'useful reading'. Lalor seems to have been genuinely interested in popular worker education and self-improvement and in 1845 he applied for a position as lecturer and librarian at the Belfast Mechanics Institute for which he solicited testimonials from several friends in the Kilkenny area. He laid his failure to be appointed 'at the door of religion'.

Lalor's attempt in his late thirties, to secure a job may have been sparked by fundamental political disagreement with his father. While several of Patrick Lalor's younger sons actively campaigned for their father on various political platforms, his eldest son did not. This may reflect some embarrassment about his personal appearance but is more likely to reflect political disagreement. Unlike his father, Lalor was extremely hostile to both Daniel O'Connell and the Repeal Movement. His hostility even went to the extent of writing a letter in 1843, Repeal Year, to British Prime Minister Sir Robert Peel, who was the Repeal Movement's most powerful enemy, offering to keep the latter informed about developments in repeal agitation. In a postscript to this letter he informed Peel that while he had one time been something more than a mere Repealer in private feeling but Mr O' Connell, his *agitators*, and his series of wretched agitations, first *disgusted* me into a conservative in point of *feeling*, and reflection and experience have *convinced* me into one in point of *principle*.

Lalor's conservatism and hostility to Repeal was primarily motivated by concern for Irish social conditions, in particular for the state of rural Ireland. Some years previously he had come into contact with the rural philosopher and economist William Conner, who lived near Athy, and there is little doubt that Conner was a formative influence on Lalor's ideas. Conner probably deserves to be remembered as the first Irish pamphleteer to denounce the iniquities of the Irish land system. In a pamphlet published in 1832, and again in his evidence to the Devon Commission in 1843, he advocated a system of setting fair rents and granting security of tenure. As Lalor did later, Conner argued that Catholic emancipation and political reform were useless without reform of the land system. Like Lalor, Conner was also highly critical of O'Connell and was thrown out of the Repeal Movement in 1843. However, while Conner believed that Repeal of the Union must predate any improvement land reform, Lalor at this stage believed, as he told Peel, 'that it was only to a Conservative Government, to her landed proprietors, and to *peace* that this country can look for any improvement in her social conditions'. To assist this end Lalor promised to keep Peel informed about the progress of the Repeal agitation, an offer Peel gratefully accepted and which apparently led to Lalor sending at least one further report to the British Prime Minister.

Lalor's split with his father and letter to Peel reflect a fundamentally different outlook on Irish society to that of O'Connell and mainline repealers. Unlike O'Connell, and also presumably his father, he was not an enthusiast for economic liberalism and the steady advance of the modern industrial age. He had apparently read many of the official inquiries into conditions in the new factories and cities; he was also an enthusiastic fan of the romantic novelist Sir Walter Scott, and like his contemporaries such as Disraeli in the Young England movement, or Friedrich Engels, he recoiled from the horrors of the new industrial age. This is how he described it in 1844:

They pass their lives from the cradle to the coffin shut up from the sun and sky and air, working in the furnace and the factory, dwelling in the filthiest lanes of a filthy town, amid everything that is most offensive and disgusting and revolting, an abomination to human feelings and human senses.

He utterly rejected any idea that the future of Ireland lay in developing an industrial sector, particularly industries dependent on exports. The future of Ireland, he informed Irish landowners in an address written in 1844, in language which could have come straight from a novel of Sir Walter Scott, lay in creating 'a peasantry, not breeders of stock or feeders of fat cattle; not gentlemen who try to be farmers nor farmers who try to be gentlemen' but 'a numerous plain and home-bred yeomanry', and he looked to the landlords to bring this about by means of enlightened estate management and some form of tenant right, possibly on the lines recommended in the report of the Devon Commission or the writings of the Ulster tenant-right leader, Sharman Crawford.

Much of this vision was shared by the Young Irelanders who also saw the landlords as the natural leaders of Irish society, however they differed from Lalor in giving priority to political rather than social reform,

Lalor's idealized vision was destroyed by two related factors: the repeal of the Corn Laws in 1846 which spelled the end of intensive tillage, ushering in the era of cattle farming, and the event which sparked the repeal of the Corn Laws – the Great Famine. He was among the first to realize that the Famine had brought about a social revolution with 'a deeper social disorganization than did the French revolution'.

It has unsettled society to the foundation; deranged every interest, every class, every household. Everyman's place and relation is altered; labour has left its track and life lost its form. One entire class, the most numerous and important in Ireland has already begun to give way; and is about being displaced. The tenant-farmer of ten acres or under is being converted into an 'independent labourer'.

The survival of a strong tenant-farmer class was Lalor's major concern. It is perhaps worth pointing out that Lalor showed no specific interest in the plight of agricultural labourers, his concern is with the ranks of the tenant farmer, a group he sees as the back bone of the nation. His main concern is to prevent a decline in the number of tenant farmers or their transformation into labourers, Despite James Connolly's enthusiasm for his ideas, he was by no means a socialist, indeed until 1847 Lalor is most accurately described as a conservative who saw the landlords as the natural leaders of society and sought a more benevolent involvement from them in improving the lot of the peasantry.

Despite his awareness of the social revolution being brought about by the Famine, Lalor was slow to lose faith in the landlords and he still clung for some time to the hope that they would help save the Irish tenant farmers. In this he was not alone; in

December 1846 O'Connell planned to unite landlords and the Irish middle class in a great national confederation. When the Young Irelanders broke with O'Connell in January 1847 to found the Irish Confederation, they too believed in the need to unite all Irishmen, including landlords and farmers, in a national movement.

Now that they had broken with O'Connell, Lalor was interested in becoming involved with the Young Irelanders. His first piece published in *The Nation* was a reprint of his 1844 appeal to the Irish landlords, and he followed this up with yet another in April 1847. Yet Lalor, though slow to lose faith in the landlords, did so much sooner than the majority of Young Irelanders. The mass evictions and horrors of the Poor Law during the Famine years provided evidence of obvious landlord indifference to the plight of the peasants. Lalor's message of April 1847 to the landlords contained an undoubted ultimatum. They can either declare their allegiance to Ireland and work with the peasants to rebuild a new and better social order and a new agrarian system based on a strong and prosperous peasantry, or else they will face a popular struggle. By this stage Lalor was suggesting a mass rent strike by the Irish tenantry in an effort to undermine the landlord system, but this idea proved too radical for the Young Irelanders, even for John Mitchel.

In June 1847 Lalor wrote to Mitchel protesting about Young Ireland's continued interest in involving the landlords and doubting whether he could still consider himself a member of the Irish Confederation. Lalor stated that he had no interest in the landlord and tenant question as commonly understood and, in one of his most quoted phrases, announced that his interest was not in repealing the Union but the Conquest:

That the absolute ownership of the lands of Ireland is vested of right in the people of Ireland – that they, and none but they, are the first landowners and lords paramount as well as the lawmakers of this island – that all titles to land are invalid if not conferred or confirmed by them – and that no man has a right to hold one foot of Irish soil otherwise than by grant of tenancy and fee from them. ... these are my principles.

What all this means in practice is obscure and open to numerous interpretations. Despite its radical tones it did not imply land nationalisation in socialist terms. Lalor continues,

To such landowners as could be brought to recognize this right of the Irish people and to swear allegiance to this island-Queen, I would grant new titles. Those who might refuse should cease to be landowners or quit this land, and their lands be vested in the occupying tenants.

This suggests either tenant right, or peasant ownership of land, nothing more radical. This is to some extent confirmed by Lalor's next move. By the summer of 1847 Lalor, disappointed at the conservatism of the Young Irelanders, had turned his attention from what was happening in Dublin and set out to organize a grass-roots tenant right movement. There was already some stirring of tenant right groups in County Cork. Lalor now threw himself into the establishment of a tenant right movement in County Tipperary rather than in his native Laois, because of the hostility of his father. He wrote to Dr Slattery, archbishop of Cashel, seeking his approval but his only supporter among the clergy was Father John Kenyon. The high point, or low point, of this phase of his political career came with the holding of a tenant right meeting at Holycross, County Tipperary, in September 1847 with the aim of establishing a tenant right association. The meeting attracted considerable attention in the press but was only attended by three or four thousand people. In the resolutions proposed Lalor began with the apparently radical preamble 'that of natural right the soil of Ireland belongs to the people of Ireland' but only appears to have sought the introduction of the Ulster Custom, fixity of tenure, fair rent and freedom of sale, into Tipperary. The meeting however ended in chaos when the land reformer and Lalor's old mentor, William Conner, addressed the crowd and proceeded to disagree with Lalor over some subtle nuances of the tenant right question. This led to both parties exchanging in both verbal and physical abuse. The precise cause of disagreement remains very obscure; both appear to have shared common ideas on the land question. However, the dispute undoubtedly damaged Lalor's proposed movement and appears to have lost him the support of Young Irelander Michael Doheny. Whatever the reason, we hear no more of the Tipperary tenant rights movement. From this point on, despite the rhetoric, Lalor seems to have become a straight-forward political revolutionary.

The continuing horrors of the Famine in the autumn of 1847, and Lalor's writings, eventually converted Young Irelander John

Mitchel to the idea of combining political and social revolution. However, his efforts to persuade the other Young Irelanders to adopt even a moderate commitment to tenant right proved unsuccessful. In February 1848 the Irish Confederation announced that they would limit their campaign to securing changes in the Irish parliamentary system. With this decision Mitchel broke away to found a new newspaper, *The United Irishman*, where, in common with Lalor, he condemned the landlords and the government for criminal neglect of the Irish people. The onset of the 1848 Revolution in France led to increased militancy among Irish nationalists and greater concern on the part of the government. Mitchel was arrested in the spring of 1848 and his newspaper, *The United Irishman*, ceased publication. However, John Martin, Mitchel's brother-in-law, and Devin Reilly established another newspaper, *The Irish Felon*, to spread Mitchel's message of political and social revolution. Lalor had not been involved with Mitchel's newspaper, however Martin and Reilly sought his assistance with *The Irish Felon* and this short-lived revolutionary newspaper published virtually all Lalor's later writings.

These reiterate and refine the political message which Lalor had already preached in the pages of *The Nation*: that the land of Ireland belonged to the people of Ireland, his interest not in Repeal but in absolute independence, and in a combination of political and social reform. He was strongly of the opinion that moral force alone was useless without military support and further that the people of Ireland would not rebel to achieve Repeal. He suggested therefore that Repeal should be linked to a more popular course, 'like a railway carriage to a train', and the popular cause he suggested was land reform. To achieve both land reform and independence Lalor proposed a programme of rent strikes, mass resistance to eviction and pressure to determine fair rents. It is not perhaps surprising, given the unstable situation throughout Europe and its revolutionary message, that *The Irish Felon* was suppressed and its editor John Martin arrested. At this stage Lalor shows himself to have certain aspirations towards political martyrdom. He wrote to Dublin Castle informing the authorities that he was the author of the inflammatory articles for which John Martin had been arrested. However, Lalor was not arrested, nor was he chosen as one of the five leaders for the uprising which was then being planned. As a consolation he set off for Tipperary and Limerick in the company of two subsequent founders of the Fenians, Thomas Clarke Luby and John O'Leary, to organize potential rebels. He missed out on the 1848 rising but was arrested and spent some months in prison only to be released at the end of 1848 due to poor health. Once released, Lalor resumed contact with those potential rebels who had remained free and became involved in an oath-bound revolutionary cell which bears a striking resemblance to the later Fenian Brotherhood. This group planned yet another uprising in 1849 and in preparation Lalor bought himself a telescope and railway map and headed back to County Tipperary where, alas, few rebels were to be found though an abortive attack took place on Cappoquin police station. Following this fiasco Lalor returned to Dublin where he died some months later.

There is little doubt that Lalor's immediate impact on Irish nationalism was negligible. With the possible exception of Mitchel, neither the nationalist leadership nor the mass of the Irish people was converted to his opinions and during the Famine years the Irish land question proved a futile issue as Lalor's abortive ventures in trying to establish a Tipperary tenant-right movement bear out. Most of Lalor's political associates, including the future Fenians Luby and O'Leary, were frankly sceptical about his political and social vision. It was only in later generations, when the immediate threat of famine had lifted and a greater political sophistication had developed, that Lalor's analysis bore fruit. His view of the land question as the engine to draw the Repeal train is virtually a blue print for the New Departure of the 1870s, as are his ideas about resisting eviction and no-rent campaigns.

At another level the picture emerges of a desperately ill man determined at all costs to perform some gesture of national significance. He seems to have had certain difficulties in working with others and there is little doubt that by 1848 he possessed a martyr complex as is shown in his efforts to have himself arrested by writing to Dublin Castle. The mass of the people had shown little interest in his message, but despite this he was determined to strike a blow. In 'Clearing the decks', the last piece he published in *The Irish Felon*, Lalor wrote:

It is never the mass of a people that forms its real and efficient might. It is the men by whom that mass is moved and managed. All the great acts of history have been done by a very few men.

He concludes:

Meanwhile, however, remember this – that somewhere, and somehow and by somebody, a beginning must be made. Who strikes the first blow for Ireland? Who draws first blood for Ireland? Who wins a wreath that will be green for ever?

The records of the National Library show that Patrick Pearse read this article on his final visit to the library in the early months of 1916. The parallels with Pearse's 'blood sacrifice' are obvious. Both men had failed to transmit their message to a popular audience, both were desperate for some form of success. Lalor may therefore be responsible not only for injecting the land question into Irish nationalism, but for prompting the highly susceptible Patrick Pearse to strike the first blow.

FURTHER READING

The only worthwhile biography of Lalor is T.P. O Neill's *Fiontan O Leathlobhair* (Dublin 1962). Kevin B. Nowlan, *The Politics of Repeal* (London 1965), is valuable on Lalor's relations with Young Ireland. The social and economic conditions within which Lalor wrote are described in Mary E. Daly, *The Famine in Ireland* (Dublin 1986), and in the collection of studies on *The Great Famine*, edited by T.D. Williams and R. D. Edwards (London 1956). The Lalor papers (National Library of Ireland, especially MSS 8570, 8562-3, 5756-7 and 340) are helpful on his family background. Lalor's letters to *The Nation* and *The Irish Felon* are available in two editions and both have valuable introductions. *The Writings of James Fintan Lalor, with an Introduction Embodying Personal Recollections by John O'Leary* (Dublin 1895) and Lilian Fogarty, *James Fintan Lalor; Patriot and Political Essayist, preface by Arthur Griffith* (Dublin 1918). Also of use is George O'Brien, 'William Conner', *Studies* (1923), pp. 279-89.

No. 235.   STATESMEN, No. 143.

"Home-Rule."

X

ISAAC BUTT (1813 - 79)
and the Inner Failure of Protestant Home Rule

W.J. McCORMACK

Isaac Butt was born on the 6th of September, 1813, at Glenfin, in County Donegal, the son of a not-overzealous clergyman, His was of course a settler family, and in *The Gap of Barnesmore* (1848) Butt wrote a novel about 1688, the clash of rival claimants to the land of Ireland, and the effects of civil war. The novel has been forgotten. But its author died at once renowned and rejected, at the age of sixty-five, having been ousted from leadership of the Irish party in a manoeuvre which soon transferred power to Charles Stewart Parnell. Initially, he was commemorated in the name of a swivel-bridge in Dublin, and though this was later replaced by a substantial stone structure, Butt's monument is overshadowed by a metal railway and, more recently, by the city's first sky-scraper. In life, and after it, Isaac Butt had been a difficult man to decipher. It is fair to say that he was a transitional figure in Irish political life, linking the period of Daniel O'Connell's last campaign for repeal of the Union to the heady days of Parnellite obstruction. But it is also necessary to appreciate the range of interests, prejudices, talents and liabilities which Butt possessed – or was possessed by – in the course of his public life. I will look first at Butt's career, and then turn to his writings in search of some pattern or imagery to illuminate his failure. Instead of a history of Isaac Butt, something more like a cultural diagnosis of loss may emerge. Through that, we may be able to discern some characteristic *mentalités* of the social constituency which Butt symbolized, essentially the professional classes of Victorian Ireland dominated still (but insecurely) by Protestants.

After an upbringing marked by all the comic indignities of genteel poverty, Isaac Butt entered public life at a precociously early age. Educated at the Royal School, Raphoe, he won first place in the entrance examination to Trinity College, Dublin, at the age of fifteen. Catholic emancipation was legislated in 1829 and the Reform Act followed three years later. Butt found himself in the company of disillusioned young men, Tory in their politics and angry at their party's compliance with demands for emancipation. From this inauspicious cabal emerged *The Dublin University Magazine*, and from 1833 the *DUM* was for forty years Ireland's most substantial literary and political journal. The following year Butt himself took control and edited the magazine for four years during which time he became prominent in the sub-world of Dublin journalism, linked to the legal profession by his official studies and to conservative politics by his penchant for controversy.

In 1837 Butt briefly embraced yet another possible muse, the patroness of academic groves, when he was appointed professor of Political Economy in the University of Dublin at the age of twenty-three. The chair, established in 1832 for a succession of five-year incumbents, was far from being a permanent university post. In a cumbersome annotation of his inaugural lecture, however, Butt alluded to a mode of thinking (or philosophical anxiety) which was to presist with him until his death:

When the mind reflects for a moment on the question of materiality or immateriality of some products, perhaps it may appear that to attempt to decide the point, would involve all the subtleties of the Berkeleyan system of Idealism. (*An Introductory Lecture* ... Dublin 1837. p. 60.)

This central issue of George Berkeley's system recurs in Butt's writings throughout his career, even at moments of personal and professional triumph, for reasons scarcely discernible in the 1830s.

By the spring of 1840 he had built up a substantial legal practice, and was regarded as the champion of Irish Protestant conservatism. O'Connell was determined to break the Protestant monopoly in municipal politics, and Butt led the rearguard action against reform, fulminating repeatedly about the dangers of a 'popish ascendancy' should Catholics be admitted to the corporations. Bitter things were said on all sides, but few more bitter than the things said by Isaac Butt. At a meeting in the Dublin Mansion House in February 1840 he claimed that a priest, Father Thomas O'Brien Costello, had sworn he could return the devil himself for the constituency of Limerick if he, Costello, wanted to. Details of such performances can be traced in Butt's *Irish Municipal Reform* (Dublin 1840, see esp. p. 25).

The explanations usually offered of Butt's transformation from Orange firebrand to Home Rule leader involve problems. The first, a general rule of transformation as we might call it, is encapsulated in the title and motto of Terence de Vere White's valuable biography, *The Road of Excess* (Dublin 1946). According to this way of thinking, the very excesses of Butt's early politics somehow guaranteed the wisdom of his middle-age. Yet though one could argue that the later Butt was a more moderate man – *politically* – than the incendiary of 1840, he can hardly be said to have been successful – unless a swivel bridge is the proper reward for success. Nor can one see in Butt's House of Commons performance in the years before party rivals engineered his fall anything quite like wisdom. No, for all that 'The Road of Excess' derives from the poetry of William Blake, the general rule of transformation is just an abstract statement of the more familiar Irish belief that all men are capable of seeing the wisdom of *my* ways – and no more so than that curious, discontinuous and yet persistent line of Protestant endorsers of the national ideal who, if they do not embrace popular tradition, decline to interrogate it. Butt's real sponsors were intermittent voices of this kind; and in this way, the legitimacy of 'my ways' was extended.

The second explanation for Butt's change of course is more strictly professional. Highly gifted as a barrister, he came to defend nationalist prisoners in 1848 and again in the 1860s. Always short of money, Butt took the best cases, and in mid-nineteenth-century Ireland the best cases lay with the nationalist prisoners. This explanation could be developed along either of two lines: either that Butt was drawn from professional association with nationalists into political association with them; or, alternatively, that he chose nationalist politics because it looked more like being a winner in the end.

The problems are obvious enough. If 1848 brought Butt into active defence of nationalists, how is it that, in the same year, he stood as a Tory for the parliamentary seat of Mayo; and that he entered parliament as member for Harwich? De Vere White's biography may argue that 'The Road of Excess Leads to the Palace of Wisdom'. But what wisdom can one find in Butt's lackadaisical parliamentary manner? Finally, and more substantially, was Butt's later position ever *nationalist* in the sense used of Young Irelanders or Fenians? Did Butt change, or is there an underlying consistency in the positions he adopted?

In 1852 he left Ireland for Westminster, for a practice at the English bar, and the begetting of several illegitimate children. He soon had to contest a general election, choosing this time to stand for Youghal where he ran into strong opposition from Catholic clergy, and finally winning by just two votes. In his biographer's view, Butt was effectively returned by the Protestant voters in Youghal and opposed by the Catholic. His next moment of national fame came with the Fenian trials. Yet these brought little financial reward by way of fees, and not only did Butt's clients all end up serving lengthy sentences, Butt himself was promptly jailed for debt and spent the best part of eighteen months in the Dublin Marshalsea and Kilmainham Gaol.

Two details from the circumstances of his last days in Kilmainham and his subsequent involvement in Home Rule politics should be rescued from obscurity. His clerk recorded how Butt, while still in gaol and with a good twelve years to live, contemplated the appropriate circumstances for his own funeral – he insisted that rain should fall persistently throughout the interment. Of course, he knew the Donegal climate well and could rely on this atmospheric detail. Nevertheless, we should note that melancholy frequently marked Isaac Butt as her own, despite his ability to recover from financial and domestic set-backs. On his release from prison, he began to write on Irish economic problems, and the title of one of these publications – *The Irish Querist: a Series of Questions, Proposed for the Consideration of all who Desire to Solve the Problem of Ireland's Social Condition* (Dublin 1867) – deserves examination. Indeed, such localized attention to detail in Butt's miscellaneous writings may serve as a better indicator of his cast of mind and its impingement on the material condition of Ireland than a calendar of dates and debates.

An understanding of Butt's espousal of Home Rule from 1870 onwards, and the failure of his campaign to carry fellow-Protestants with him, requires a reconsideration of his writings from as early as 1833. The Home Government Association of 1870 was largely the work of Dublin professional men, many of them Protestant by denomination. Just as the *DUM* launched him in the first place, these were the sponsors of Isaac Butt's return to politics. In essence, Butt's biography does not so much demonstrate transformation and development as it exemplifies a curiously prolific range of stances, each obstructing or obscuring the central aspect of his identity – its immobility, its persistent concentration on the problem of the relation between inner and outer worlds, its ultimate (I believe) scepticism on the reality of a categorical distinction between the inner and the outer.

The title of *The Irish Querist* was frankly borrowed from George Berkeley's more famous *Querist* of 1735-7. In a volume in the National Library of Ireland containing Butt's *Querist* there is a manuscript note in the hand of one to whom Butt had given the five pamphlets bound therein; it reads 'He was particularly proud of the "Irish Querist" and set great store by it. ... 'Why did Isaac Butt call his pamphlet *The Irish Querist*, for Berkeley's pamphlet had been an Irish querist – it dealt explicitly with Ireland, its social condition, and the economic solutions which might be adopted? There is in Butt's title a characteristic over-emphasis, an inner oscillation or tautology which is symptomatic. The point is not as finicky as might be imagined. Butt had a decidedly intense relationship with Bishop Berkeley, from whom he claimed a kind of descent through his mother. His mother's Christian name was Berkeley – she had been Miss Berkeley Cox, to be exact – and Butt gave *two* of his children this same Christian name. Query 247 of Butt's publication refers to Berkeley himself and *his* querist, a feature which gives Isaac something of the air of a man composing jeremiads about Jeremiah! Furthermore, in 1865 Butt delivered a public lecture in Dublin on 'Bishop Berkeley and his Writings', and this is published in the *Afternoon Readings* series. There is a rational link between Berkeley and Butt – the latter was an ardent protectionist in his economic views, and Berkeley could be interpreted as a protectionist before the event. Indeed, back in the 1840s during his Orange days, Butt's protectionist principles led him to cooperate with O'Connell in campaigns concerning Irish trade. However, there was also a non-rational element in Butt's fixation with Berkeley, and it is an aspect of his psyche which may be discovered through other means.

Isaac Butt was prolific all his life, his publications commencing with translations of Ovid and Virgil published in 1833 and 1834 when he was twenty-one. Through *The Dublin University Magazine* and through more ephemeral newspapers, he also wrote a great deal of journalism on matters of some and no importance. Among his contributions to the *DUM* the most significant was a lengthy article entitled 'Past and Present State of Literature in Ireland' published in 1837. This is the first attempt to examine the theoretical base for a distinctive Anglo-Irish literature, and one of its most striking features is Butt's emphasis on the impact of printing, the significance of different technologies and economies of publication in Britain and Ireland. Behind the obvious political arguments there lies a highly original concern for the relation between communications (as we would say today) and culture. In particular, Butt concentrates on the qualitative change effected by the expansion of readership to encompass the masses, or at least the bulk of the middle classes. Steam-powered printing on the one hand, and vanity publication on the other, give rise (in Butt's words) to 'the vast production of works which have no circulation and no readers' (*DUM* vol 9, March 1837, p. 368). And even in his notes to the *Georgics* he goes to the trouble of reminding the late Edward Gibbon that print-technology did not exist in Virgil's Rome.

Nearly forty years later, Butt published a lecture which he had delivered at the Limerick Athenaeum on 1 October 1872, *Intellectual Progress* (Limerick 1872). He was by now MP for Limerick – perhaps he was the very devil Fr Costello had threatened. He certainly was the prominent advocate of a new Home Rule policy, soon to have sixty followers behind him at Westminster. (Or, more often, ahead of him!) His lecture repeated his concern with the impact of the press on culture and the dissemination of information, with the arrival of the steam-boat, the railways, and the telegraph, though by now he approved popular access to knowledge and no longer echoed S. T. Coleridge's anxiety on the topic. As in his earlier lecture on Bishop Berkeley, he included a proper allowance of Victorian sentiment. We are fortunate that the library in Trinity College, Dublin, preserves a copy of this lecture annotated by Butt himself, and the most striking annotation comes in the course of the following paragraph:

What voices of sorrow speak to our hearts in the moaning of the gusts of the night wind as they pass. What hidden chords of our inner being are touched by the mournful melody of that sound. All our inner being vibrates to something in the eternal world which the perceptions of sense cannot reveal. (p. 24)

Maybe there is no more to this than a re-run of Butt's anticipation of rainy burial. Nevertheless, he took care to correct a word in that apparently banal sentence about the inner being vibrating to the eternal world so that it reads, in the annotated copy: 'All our inner being vibrates to something in the external [sic] world which the perceptions of sense cannot reveal.'

All of a sudden, banality has turned into a far more puzzling expression. Butt evidently questions the ability of our sense perceptions to get to grips with the *external* world. Such concerns occasionally characterized writing as distinguished as Sterne's and Wordsworth's, and the slight correction to a presentation copy of his lecture economically indicates Butt's casual participation in a philosophical debate reaching back into the eighteenth century. For a rather over-simplified reading of George Berkeley's finely wrought philosophy might be summarized in not dissimilar terms. Though analogical arguments require more detail than can be provided here and now, we can suggest that, in the grosser world of Victorian Britain, the relation between print-technology and culture reproduced the same problem, the questionable ability of the apparatus of books, newspapers, telegraphs, to sustain a relationship with those values we call culture. The vast production of books which had no readers and no circulation, which Butt described in 1837, is an image of non-communication, in which no human subject perceives the products of human industry. Conversely, the tautology of *The Irish Querist* as a title – the *Querist* itself had been Irish in a quite straightforward way – is an image of the subject becoming the object of its own perception, not in reflexive self-consciousness, but more in the manner in which facing mirrors endlessly reproduce their contents without altering them.

These are fairly dry-as-dust ways of characterizing a politician's career, and some effort must now be made to bring them into contact with the great issues of Butt's public life. His economic theories form a useful bridge-head between philosophical conundrums and matters of incontrovertible fact. Butt was, as I have said, a protectionist. That is, he believed that a system of tariffs and taxes should be employed to protect industry, sustain employment, and stabilize prices. Politically, his commitment to protection (which had been evident early in the 1840s when he co-operated with O'Connell) became crucial in 1845 when Sir Robert Peel decided to repeal the Corn Laws and so end protection of agriculture. The Irish context (and pretext) for this drastic innovation was of course the Famine, and Butt wrote bitterly:

To profess belief in the fact of the existence of a formidable potato blight
was as sure a method of being branded as a radical as to propose to destroy
the [Established] Church. (*A Voice for Ireland*, Dublin 1847, p.3.)

Butt's deeply emotional personality was traumatized by the
Famine and the consequences of the blight, and he did not yield in
his commitment to protection even if it resulted in his appearing to
be a radical like Fintan Lalor or a repealer like William Smith
O'Brien. Indeed the very surplus of emotion which he displayed is
an indicator of the barriers between experience and the outer
world, barriers which structured his psyche.

The fundamental basis of protectionism, however, is the
economic entity to be protected, and usually the nation-state served
that purpose. For Butt, as a Unionist, Ireland could never be a
nation-state. Yet, as his article on Anglo-Irish literature had shown,
he was well aware of the economic, technical, and cultural
discrepancies of development subsisting between Britain and
Ireland. Within Ireland, Butt also had a series of what I call social
constituencies - the Protestant malcontents who founded *The
Dublin University Magazine*, the Youghal voters who squeezed him
back into the House of Commons in 1852, and those in the Home
Government Association of 1870 like Major Laurence Knox
(proprietor of *The Irish Times*), Sir William Wilde, Professors
Galbraith and Haughton of Trinity College, and William Shaw
(President of the Munster Bank) who were Protestants. Of course,
these latter soon abandoned Butt to his unholy alliance with ex-
Fenians, a radical Presbyterian, and sundry priests. In this
connection David Thornley's intricate tracing of political
manoeuvre in *Isaac Butt and Home Rule* (London 1964) ably
complements de Vere White's biography.

What kind of entity did the Protestants of Ireland constitute?
This is the question which underlies Butt's career from the 1830s to
his death in 1879. His opposition to municipal reform in 1840 had
been based on a positive view of their claims, and this was in
keeping with the 1837 article on literary culture. However, such a
defence of the Protestants rested on a kind of protectionism, and
protectionism after the fall of the all-Protestant corporations
required a larger base. Exploiting the *ressentiment* of a middle-class
caucus which has lost its corporation monopoly, Butt brilliantly

sustained a political career of mutually gratifying compensations – the Orange firebrand defends Thomas Francis Meagher, and the professional totem-poles of Protestant Dublin will later very usefully foist Butt upon their enemies. Throughout his life Butt sought to represent (in the most comprehensive range of senses of the word 're-present') some integral entity – a client in court, a denominational monopoly, an entire people.

Such a concept of self, of a contained and articulate entity, is finally unsustainable philosophically, and leads *in extremis* to various doctrines of solipsism according to which knowledge is strictly limited to states of the knower's own self. According to the solipsist – and there can only be one of that species – nothing exists really beyond the contents of a single mind. Butt displayed traits of what one might call behavioural solipsism, as when he would deliberately talk nonsense at dinner-parties – the relationship between sardines and algebra was a favourite topic. At a more symptomatic level, this kind of drastic inwardness occurs periodically in Irish Protestant culture. It is increasingly evident in the work of Butt's friend Sheridan Le Fanu, and it is a point of departure – an oppressive legacy renounced – in the far more achieved work of J.M. Synge. Currently, Ulster Unionism is soliloquizing on its advisability or otherwise. I do not want to suggest that any inherent, quasi-racial trait is identified in this inwardness - far from it. I would, on the contrary, argue strongly that every instance of this 'Protestant culture turned in upon itself' is socially determined, and that the case of Isaac Butt illustrates the process with remarkable clarity.

After the Union conservatism in Ireland had undergone a strange transformation. A host of Irish political figures found themselves rapidly promoted through the ranks of the imperial administration. These included Lord Castlereagh who became Foreign Secretary, John Wilson Croker who became Secretary to the Admiralty and who coined the term 'conservative', George Canning and the duke of Wellington who both became Prime Minister in the 1820s. Isaac Butt entered the Irish public scene as the consequences of this evacuation became drastic. He was the first leader of Irish conservative opinion who committed himself to a career generally focused within the island of Ireland. That career fell between a phase of history defined by the Union and its immediate consequences and a later phase ultimately defined by degrees of separatist longing and separating accident. What is particularly remarkable of the mid-Victorian period is the uncertainty and lack of assurance of its political language, especially the language of a conservative ideology. The key terms of Irish nineteenth-century politics – emancipation, tenant right, repeal – belong to the other side. Union itself was a highly charged term, of course, but union evidently endorsed emancipation and (at the time of the Famine) provided no defence of Irish land.

When a social constituency lacks a confident vocabulary, and experiences a gulf between its language and the actuality of political endeavour, it finds itself in a position not unlike that of the books Butt referred to in 1837, the books without readers and without circulation. Butt himself had produced a book which probably had few readers, *The Georgics of Virgil Translated into English Prose with an Appendix of Critical and Explanatory Notes* (Dublin 1834). I believe that as early as his notes in this edition of the *Georgics*, Butt provided a covert interpretation of the relation between his middle-class, Protestant, sponsoring constituency and the language of metropolitan culture. Annotating a line early in the poem, Butt comments as follows:

This is the passage upon which Mr. Gibbon grounds his conjecture with regard to the intention of the poet in the composition of the Georgics – that they were written to reconcile the turbulent spirits of the newly settled veterans to the calm and peaceful pursuits of agriculture ... Mr Gibbon attributes to the dissemination of this poem the tranquillity that marked the latter years of Augustus's reign; but we must seek elsewhere for its causes. It must not be forgotten that Rome had no printing presses, and the circulation of the Georgics was both limited and delayed by the tedious and expensive nature of the manuscript process which attended publication. ... The political effects of literature may be sure, but they are slow, and it probably requires a generation at least to pass away before the finest efforts of genius can exercise their favourable though indirect influence upon the social system. ... Ballads have more than once produced an insurrection, but ballads have never quelled one. ... (pp. 134-5)

This may be poor classical scholarship but it is a revealing statement of the relation between planter discontent and high culture. The trouble was, as Butt's longer analysis of Irish literary prospects demonstrated, that Anglophone culture in Ireland was bedevilled by a self-consciousness of its own paucity. George Berkeley could be interpreted as glossing this fearfully unanchored activity of language in his *Theory of Vision Vindicated* (sect. 39 & 40) when he speaks of the arbitrary character of signs, including linguistic signs. Butt was just the man so to interpret his beloved ancestor, and he particularly drew attention to this pamphlet of Berkeley's in his 1865 lecture. The dictinctive term which Butt was to bequeath to the language of Irish politics – Home Rule – emphasized a domestic and middle-class locus. Ireland was a home within another world with which connections might be usefully modified – a return of power into the *home*. A search for both inwardness and connection concluded in the ultimately futile campaign for a domestic parliament.

Isaac Butt has tended to disappear behind the lines of political and historical disputes centred on apparently more substantial figures. The same sense of historical marginality, the need for qualification, has misled many lecturers to open sentences about the leader of Home Rule with the conjunction 'but' only to find that old Isaac has merged with the qualifier in an onomatapoeic putter of 'But Butt ...'. Yet even this chameleon-like invisibility is positively reflected in the many puns upon the name in *Finnegans Wake*. Isaac Butt's mortal dissolution fitted some pattern of this kind. I cannot be sure that it rained as they buried him in Stranorlar graveyard, but the officiating clergyman inexplicably refused to deliver a single word or tribute or commentary on the deceased. His lips were sealed, he said. It was a conclusion Butt might have found symptomatic on a wider scale.

FURTHER READING

Terence de Vere White's very readable *The Road Of Excess* (Dublin 1948) remains the only biography of Isaac Butt. For the general cultural background see W. J. Mc Cormack's *Sheridan Le Fanu and Victorian Ireland* (Oxford 1980). Nicholas Mansergh's *The Irish Question 1840-1921* (3rd ed. London 1975) provides a blend of political and cultural analysis which is good on mid-century romanticism, and should be read in conjunction with R. V. Comerford, *The Fenians in Context* (Dublin 1985), while R.D.C. Black's *Economic Thought and the Irish Question 1917-1870* (Cambridge 1960) provides a solid framework in which to assess Butt's economic theories. At the specifically political level, and concentrating on the final years, David Thornley's *Isaac Butt and Home Rule* (London 1964) is also recommended to more specialist inquirers.

THE IRONY OF CIRCUMSTANCE

MR JOHN REDMOND : " Well, if I can't rule in Dublin, I can here."

Reproduced from "Punch," February 2, 1910, by kind permission of the Proprietors

172

XI

JOHN REDMOND (1856-1918)
and Home Rule

MICHAEL LAFFAN

IN THE YEARS BEFORE the First World War John Redmond exercised a degree of power and influence in both Ireland and Britain which few Irish politicians had enjoyed before him. It seemed as if nothing could prevent him from achieving Home Rule, the objective which had been shared by almost all nationalists for the previous forty years. Where Butt and Parnell had both failed, he seemed destined to succeed. His followers revelled in their sense of impending triumph.

In some respects Redmond was an improbable figure to play the role of national hero. Shy, aloof, formal and ponderous, able to appeal to reason but not to instinct or emotion, an English-style country squire devoted to shooting and fishing, he was in many ways a most unrepresentative Irishman.

Viewed in a different light, his position was altogether appropriate. More than any other Irish nationalist politician he was a fervent believer in the British Empire and the role which Ireland should play in its development; he believed in the British constitution and its capacity to remedy Irish grievances; and he was a 'House of Commons man', thoroughly at home in Westminster. In the past his great-uncle and his father had both represented Wexford, and before his own election in 1881 he had worked as a parliamentary clerk. His early political career had been unruly, in the best Parnellite tradition; the day after first taking his seat he had been suspended and expelled from the Commons, and he later served a jail sentence which included a diet of bread and water. But these had been excesses of his youth, and by the 1910s he was a remote and formidable figure, exuding dignity and gravitas, described as having the appearance of a tamed and weary hawk, the face and figure of a Roman emperor. Asquith, the Prime Minister, used refer to him as 'Leviathan'. He was a powerful orator and a shrewd debater, widely respected by both colleagues and opponents. With considerable skill he had acted as chairman of an often rancorous party. He was the living embodiment of the Irish constitutional tradition.

Now, it seemed, his long years of patience, faith and optimism were about to be vindicated in the most suitable manner: by parliament's enactment of Home Rule, by the achievement of Irish nationalist demands as the result of negotiation and democratic procedure rather than as a concession to force or the threat of force. A politician who in bad times as well as in good had always played the parliamentary game, and was always punctilious in observing its rules, was now about to win according to those rules.

Redmond had persevered in unfavourable circumstances. The bleak years of the Parnellite split and the failure of the second Home Rule Bill in 1893 had been followed by a decade of unbroken Conservative government, a period symbolized by the phrase 'killing Home Rule with kindness'. His hopes of conciliating the Unionist minority had gradually been abandoned. Then, when the Liberals finally returned to power, they did so with an overwhelming parliamentary majority; no longer needing Irish votes to remain in office they concerned themselves with what they regarded as more urgent or more feasible tasks, with problems of social reform and foreign policy. Gladstone's commitment to Home Rule was not shared by his successors. Disillusionment with Redmond's methods and his lack of achievement spread throughout nationalist Ireland, and more radical groups such as Arthur Griffith's Sinn Féin emerged to challenge the Parliamentary Party.

Then, suddenly, everything changed. In 1909 Redmond's fortunes experienced a dramatic rise, soon to be followed by an even more spectacular fall. If he had been a less solid and prosaic figure the vicissitudes of these years might have provided suitable material for a novelist or a dramatist.

Fate had long been unkind to him, but as a result of circumstances totally beyond his control, of a crisis which had nothing whatever to do with Irish affairs, he was presented with precisely the opportunity which he had so long awaited. Lloyd George, the Chancellor of the Exchequer, introduced his radical

'People's Budget'. The measure was most unpopular in Ireland , not least because it imposed a heavy new tax on whiskey. But it also incited the House of Lords, for quite different reasons, to break with constitutional precedent and reject the budget, thereby bringing down the government and provoking a clash between the two Houses of Parliament. After a prolonged conflict which included two general elections in rapid succession, the Lords were defeated. The elections of January and December 1910, with their almost identical results, left Redmond and the Parliamentary Party holding the balance of power and able (at least in theory) to make or unmake governments. The Parliament Act of 1911 ended the Lords' veto on Home Rule. Redmond's position was now, unexpectedly, stronger than Parnell's had ever been.

This new situation provided difficulties as well as opportunities. However great his freedom of manoeuvre might appear to be, in practice Redmond's hands were tied. For the past quarter of a century, ever since Gladstone's conversion to Home Rule in 1885, the Liberals were the Parliamentary Party's only possible ally; it would not be in Redmond's interest to displace a lukewarm friend in favour of a cold and determined enemy. The government could be embarrassed by the Irish nationalists, but in the last resort it could call their bluff and challenge them to put it out of office. There were limits to the concessions which they could extract in return for their support. Some ministers were opposed to the prospect of introducing a new Home Rule Bill as the price of an Irish alliance, and even contemplated resignation rather than undergo the humiliation of dependence on Redmondite votes. Nonetheless an understanding was reached: the Parliamentary Party would combine with the Liberals to defeat the Lords and would then be rewarded by the introduction of a Home Rule Bill which would be assured of a safe passage through parliament.

So, in April 1912, Asquith introduced the third Home Rule Bill. Radical nationalists dismissed it as miserably inadequate, but in general it met with a fervent welcome in nationalist Ireland, both from those who (like Redmond) believed that it satisfied Irish demands, and from those who regarded it as a welcome first step or first instalment. Redmond had for long been a respected figure; now he experienced a brief period of adulation.

For the next two years British as well as Irish public life would be dominated by the Home Rule question.

Redmond's enemies denounced him as an unscrupulous blackmailer exploiting a spineless and unprincipled government, as a puppeteer who, by pulling strings, made the prime minister dance to a set of Irish jigs and reels. Cartoons portrayed him as holding the British constitution in the palm of his hand. Such attacks could only increase his popularity at home.

However, Asquith's government was not only grudging in respect of the powers which were to be transferred to a Dublin parliament; it was also prepared to modify its proposals in order to remove or to lessen the objections of Ulster Unionists. It would delay any such concession for as long as possible, until the bill was finally ready for enactment in 1914, but Redmond was left in no doubt that he would have to work hard to prevent his gains being whittled away.

Worst of all, it soon became clear that both the unionists and their Conservative allies were not prepared to follow Redmond's example; they would no longer pursue their objectives by political means when defeat seemed likely or certain. Edward Carson, the new leader of the Irish unionists, was fully prepared to carry the struggle against Home Rule outside parliament and to use whatever unconstitutional means he felt might be necessary. He warned that he and his colleagues would seize power in Belfast, and lead a rebellion against the government, unless it abandoned any thought of subjecting Ulster Unionists to the rule of their nationalist enemies.

Partly for tactical reasons, and partly out of genuine conviction that Home Rule for Ireland would lead to the disruption of the empire, the Conservative party under Bonar Law supported these plans for armed resistance. The leader of the opposition preached treason in a manner in which no other significant British politician had done for centuries.

The authorities, so adept at forestalling nationalist uprisings, seemed powerless when confronted with unionist rebels. Eventually even the British army was shown to be unreliable, and many of its most senior officers displayed greater sympathy with the Ulster Volunteers than with the king's government.

Carson was able to move the battlefield away from parliament, away from its comfortable majority of Liberal, Labour and Irish nationalist MPs, and the nature of the campaign which he waged deprived Redmond of most of the advantages which he had expected to enjoy. All his experience and prestige, all his appeals to reason, fair play and common sense, counted for little under the new rules drawn up for the occasion by Carson and Bonar Law. The votes of British and Irish MPs in Westminster were outweighed by the crates of German guns at Larne.

The Cabinet, already uneasy with its Irish alliance and terrified of rebellion and civil war, became even more anxious to reach a compromise settlement. Redmond was forced into a defensive position with no room for manoeuvre; he could do little more than dig in his heels and refuse to budge. Eventually, early in 1914, he felt obliged to give way to Asquith's pressure and he conceded the temporary exclusion from the Home Rule area of those four Ulster counties, Antrim, Down, Derry and Armagh, which contained Unionist majorities. No one on either side wanted partition, but increasingly it seemed to be the only way of avoiding the rebellion which Carson threatened.

The Unionists' readiness to resort to violence and their formation of a Volunteer force also undermined Redmond in another important respect. He rejected firmly any suggestion that he should follow their example, and he dismissed the argument that if Carson had strengthened his hand by his leadership of a private army, he, Redmond, could do the same, could cancel Carson's advantage, and could restore the earlier balance, by building up a rival army of his own. His position as the government's responsible, democratic ally prohibited any such move. He would squander years or decades of work if he conformed so readily to British stereotypes of the rebellious Irishman.

Unlike Parnell, he had no taste or talent for appealing to the hillside men. Oliver MacDonagh has summed up the contrast between the two nationalist leaders in these terms: Parnell first outmanoeuvred, then tamed and deployed the forces of violence; Redmond first underestimated them, then allowed them to seize the initiative. But Redmond's fear of unleashing the forces of the deep was to be vindicated by later events. Private armies, and the habit of rebellion, tended to spread; Carson's example could not be undone or forgotten.

Many other Irish nationalists felt no such inhibitions. They were excited by the Unionists' successful defiance of the government and scornful of what they viewed as Redmond's timidity. Under the influence of elements within the IRB the Irish

Volunteers were formed in 1913 and this new force soon attracted tens of thousands of young men into its ranks.

The balance between moderate and radical nationalists moved up and down like a see-saw. The initiative had moved away from Redmond during the barren years before the budget crisis and the resulting parliamentary deadlock; then it swung back towards constitutionalism as he was able to extract a Home Rule Bill from the government; and now it tilted towards extremism once again as the Irish Volunteers seemed to offer a more effective counterweight to the Ulster Unionists that the Parliamentary Party could provide. Redmond was being squeezed by Carson on the one hand and the IRB on the other. He became increasingly dependent on a prompt achievement of Home Rule to vindicate his policy and revive his followers' enthusiasm yet again.

Negotiations continued throughout the summer of 1914, but were interrupted in their closing stages by the sudden outbreak of the First World War. In order to prevent any distraction from the war effort a compromise solution was imposed. It was broadly favourable to Redmond. Home Rule became law, but its implementation would be postponed until after the end of the war and until after new legislation would be enacted to deal with the unsolved problem of Ulster.

The Ulster Volunteers had effectively deprived Redmond of the united Ireland which he and other nationalists had always naively taken for granted. And the outbreak of war in August 1914, a fluke accident of timing, deprived him of the chance to exploit his partial victory. Had the international crisis been delayed by even a few weeks, events in Ireland might well have taken a different direction.

The war undermined Redmond's position in another and less obvious sense. He supported Britain's struggle against Germany just as vehemently as, at the turn of the century, he had opposed her campaign against the Boers in South Africa. He urged Irishmen to join the British army and to fight, as he put it, 'wherever the firing line extends, in defence of right, of freedom and of religion in this war'. Some of his colleagues, especially John Dillon, were dismayed by his self-imposed role of national recruiting sergeant. But at least in the short run he retained most of his popularity; when the Irish Volunteers split, 170,000 men followed Redmond while only 10,000 remained loyal to the original leaders, Eoin MacNeill and the IRB men behind him.

Contrary to expectations, the war dragged on and on, the lists of casualties lengthened, and there was no sign either of victory or of Home Rule. Disillusionment with Redmond and his methods became more widespread.

Further misfortune followed. The Easter Rising was as much a blow at the Parliamentary Party and what it stood for as it was an attack on the British government. The Irish Solicitor General, observing the fighting, remarked 'the man I am sorry for is John Redmond'.

Some years earlier Carson had seized the initiative from him by threatening and planning rebellion. Now Clarke, Pearse and their colleagues did so again by following and surpassing Carson's example, by actually staging a rebellion. Redmond reacted with what he described as 'horror, discouragement, almost despair', and repudiated what he saw as 'the insanity of a small section of the Irish people'. Yet in private he repeatedly urged Asquith to show mercy and to stop the executions; he even threatened to resign as party leader.

After the Rising Irish nationalist opinion began, very slowly, to change. Redmond could not change with it, and he did not wish to do so. He remained faithful both to his ultimate aim of Home Rule and to his means of achieving it: negotiating with the British government. Surprisingly the Rising appeared to give him a fresh chance; the Cabinet, jolted out of its complacency towards Ireland, authorised a new round of discussions to see if a settlement could be reached. In a desperate attempt to secure Home Rule before it was too late, before Irish public opinion would reject it as inadequate, Redmond was prepared to sacrifice (at least in the short term) the two counties of Fermanagh and Tyrone for which he had fought tenaciously not long before. When the negotiations collapsed he denounced the government for its bad faith, but nationalist Ireland blamed him and his party for having been outmanoeuvred and deceived.

The result of these discussions was fatal to the parliamentarians' morale, and Redmond's own tendency to despair was revealed by his reaction to a by-election defeat in Roscommon the following year. He intended releasing to the press a defeatist memorandum in which he admitted that the people might have grown tired 'of the monotony of being served for twenty, thirty, thirty five or even forty years by the same men in Parliament, and desire variety and change'. If that were so, he would make no complaint. His horrified colleagues persuaded him not to release the document. But by this time Redmond, although only sixty years old, was ill, despondent and ageing rapidly. He had never been a gregarious man and now he became even more isolated and reclusive. The real Ireland seemed increasingly alien to him, and he made no serious effort to combat the new Sinn Féin Party.

Yet the habits of a lifetime could not be broken. In 1917 Lloyd George summoned a convention to discuss and advise on Irish affairs, and Redmond felt obliged to join in this vain enterprise, to carry on negotiating, making further concessions to the Unionists' fears and interests in the hope that he might, even at his late hour, secure Home Rule and avoid partition. Here, too, he failed.

Providence, which had treated Redmond so capriciously, first raising him up and then hurling him down, was at least merciful in sparing him the final débâcle. He died only weeks before the conscription crisis of 1918 which exposed yet more of his weaknesses and further vindicated his critics. Griffith had always claimed that the aim of holding the parliamentary balance of power was an illusion, and that when British interests were seriously threatened Liberals and Conservatives would combine at the expense of Irish nationalists; that five hundred Britons would always outvote one hundred Irishmen. In April 1918 the overwhelming majority of British MPs voted to impose conscription on Ireland, and the Parliamentary Party, its protests ignored, was reduced to implementing Sinn Féin policy, withdrawing from Westminster and returning to carry on the fight in Ireland.

Eight months later it was routed by Sinn Féin in the general election which followed the end of the war. Only six of its MPs limped back to Westminster. The party later revived in Northern Ireland where it remained the dominant voice of the nationalist minority for another fifty years, but in the South it soon became little more that a faint memory, its successes largely ignored, its failures serving only to illuminate the achievements of its enemies.

The Treaty gave the new Free State vastly greater freedom than had been on offer under Home Rule. Bloodshed extracted more concessions (or at least secured them more quickly) than the peaceful means which Redmond refused to abandon. Within a few years of his death, as Republicans and Free Staters fought a bitter civil war, the man who had for nearly twenty years been the leading figure in Irish public life was quite forgotten, his objectives overtaken by the course of events and discarded as irrelevant to the new Ireland. More than seventy years later his house in Aughavanagh in the Wicklow mountains, now an An Oige Youth Hostel, still bears no plaque in his memory.

Redmond is a tragic figure. His strength and his skills equipped him perfectly for the part which, with luck, he could be called upon to play. He *was* lucky, but not for long. For a few years he re-enacted Parnell's triumphs, inspiring vast audiences with hope and fear as he occupied the centre of the political stage. But while he was in mid-performance Carson re-wrote the script; the morality play became a melodrama dominated by guns and drums; the symbolic figures of Ulster and Eire overshadowed those who appealed for rational compromise; the leading role which he had waited half a lifetime to play dwindled to that of a plaintive chorus.

Redmond lived in a narrow and rarefied world, moderate, balanced and reasonable. Both his principles and his limitations prevented him from understanding, let alone exploiting, others whose aims and methods differed radically from is own. Carson's extremism, and the idealism and ferocity which he unleashed, evoked a response among both republicans and unionists which swept Redmond aside. With the benefit of hindsight we can see the fragility of his position and the ease with which it was undermined, but we must not forget how close he came to his goal. Chance and exceptional misfortune were necessary to make Redmond one of the great losers in Irish history.

FURTHER READING

No biography of Redmond has appeared since Denis Gwynn, *John Redmond* (London 1932). In part this neglect is a reflection of taste and fashion, but it is also a tribute to Gwynn's effective use of and quotation from Redmond's papers in the National Library of Ireland. Paul Bew, *Conflict and Conciliation in Ireland, 1890-1910* (Oxford 1987), examines aspects of his first decade as party leader, while the Home Rule crisis of 1910-14 and the decline of the Irish Parliamentary Party are discussed in Stephen Gwynn, *John Redmond's Last Years* (London 1919), Patricia Jalland, *The Liberals in Ireland: The Ulster Question in British Politics before 1914* (London 1980), and Michael Laffan, *The Partition of Ireland 1911-1925* (Dublin 1983). George Dangerfield's useful survey *The Damnable Question: A study of Anglo-Irish Relations (London 1977)* does not equal his *The Strange Death of Liberal England* (London 1935, reissued 1966, 1970, reprinted 1972, 1973) which, for all its wilfulness, remains a classic. Inevitably, Redmond features prominently in F.S.L. Lyons's valuable biography of his rival, colleague and successor *John Dillon* (London 1969). On the interaction of British and Irish politics in the years before the First World War there is much useful material in two other biographies: Roy Jenkins, *Asquith* (London 1964) and Robert Blake, *The Unknown Prime Minister: The Life and Times of Andrew Bonar Law* (London 1955).

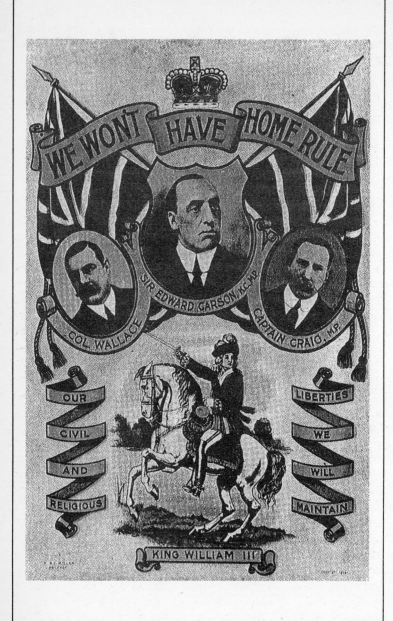

XII

EDWARD CARSON (1854-1935)
and Irish Unionism

D. G. BOYCE

AMONG THE LOSERS IN Ireland's history, Edward Carson surely counts as one of the greatest. Losers here mean not simply politicians who made mistakes – all of them do that – but those who had an alternative vision of Irish society, one which could not prevail against the tide. Carson fought for three great causes in his political life: the prosperity of his native land; the integrity of the British Isles as a single political unit; and the welfare of the British empire, that (to him) great civilizing force. These causes were in Carson's view inseparable, and what held them together, what provided their connecting link, was the presence of a strong loyal population in Ireland. If one of these causes fell, then all fell. This explains both the breadth of his design and the totality of his loss.

Let us consider the Ireland, and the Britain, that Carson fought to preserve. He was born in 1854 into a typical southern Irish Protestant background that was professional and middle-class, for while his people were led by, and closely identified with, the landed gentry, they were not as is commonly supposed all landlords. Carson's grandfather was a general merchant in Dublin; his father became an architect; his two uncles were clergymen in the Church of Ireland; his mother's family were the Lamberts of Athenry in County Galway. After school at Portarlington, Carson took a degree in Trinity College, Dublin, followed by a professional career at the Irish bar. He was called to the bar in 1877, at first earning an honest, but modest, living. By 1899 his fees at the English bar came to £20,000 a year, evidence not of Anglo-Irish privilege but of Carson's own ability (most famously demonstrated in the prosecution of his fellow-undergraduate, Oscar Wilde, in 1895).

Carson always described himself as a 'Liberal Unionist', that is one of those who were liberal or even radical in their general political convictions, but who felt that at all costs the union between Britain and Ireland must be preserved. In November 1885, while still a Liberal, he supported a Unionist parliamentary candidate because he thought it best for Ireland, warning also that the Parnellites were only concerned to catch the votes of the farmers but cared nothing for the working men of Dublin. Carson's liberalism was finally forced into a Unionist mould in 1886 because of the bolt from the blue that was Gladstone's first Home Rule Bill; and his experience as a barrister over the following years confirmed in him the view that the United Kingdom, and especially Ireland, was fast approaching the crisis of its fate. It was one thing to do the ordinary rounds of the Irish law courts, where T.M. Healy and John Redmond were his contemporaries; it was quite another to stand in the forefront of the legal and political struggles of the Plan of Campaign in 1887-88, with its catalogue of mass meetings, strident denunciation of landlords and popular defiance. Carson in later life grimly recalled the atmosphere in which he practised these legal politics: 'I remember the old Land League times and I had something to do with the administration of the law at the time when the murders which then disgraced the country went on ... I remember it all very well' (Colvin, *Carson*, iii, pp. 385-6).

Carson was no doubt exaggerating the element of violence in the Land League days; for the land war, so called, was more of a legal war, fought largely in the courts, with the British government striving to outwit, and often being outwitted by, its opponents. Nevertheless, Carson was in the thick of this legal battle. A.J. Balfour, Chief Secretary for Ireland, marked him out as a cool and determined Crown prosecutor; and when Carson was elected Unionist MP for Trinity College, Dublin, in 1892 Balfour rewarded him with the post of Solicitor-General for Ireland. 'I made Carson', he claimed, 'and Carson made me' (McDowell, 'Carson', p. 88).

But no one needed to manufacture Carson's Unionism. His experience in the Plan of Campaign only confirmed his belief that the guarantor of law, order, liberty and life in Ireland was the British connection. This was not just one-way traffic, for Carson also believed that Ireland was as important to Britain as Britain was to Ireland, and that the bond that must not be dissolved was loyal Ireland, the Ireland of crown and harp, the Ireland of 'Wellington, of Roberts, of White of Ladysmith': the whole host of the famous who had contributed to England's glory. To protect this Ireland from the Conservative policy of 'killing Home Rule with kindness' Carson fought against the central plan of buying out the Irish landlords by means of Land Purchase Acts, which he believed was both a surrender to crime and an ignoble desertion by Britain of her loyal Irish people.

Britain had the capacity to help Ireland, especially to bring her prosperity, stability and the benefits of British civilization; Ireland had the means to help Britain. 'What', Carson asked in 1912, 'is the object of the United Kingdom? As I understand it, it is that all parts shall be worked together as a whole, and with the object that the poorer may be helped by the richer, and richer may be the stronger by the co-operation of the poorer' (Colvin, p. 115) But (as in any marriage), both partners could also play a destructive role, one that Carson sought to prevent. Britain could destroy Ireland by granting Home Rule to Irish Nationalist agitators; Ireland could damage Britain because these Nationalists sought only one end, 'The dismemberment of the Empire', and once given self-government they would work ceaselessly to that end.

What was the Ireland for which Carson did fight, the Ireland that he did not seek to create? He did not strive to preserve Protestant bigotry in Ireland. Because Protestantism was loyal he defended it: but he defended it on liberal grounds as well, for it was, he believed, the guarantor of civil and religious liberty in Ireland, for all Irishmen. He understood the feelings and sought to promote the interests of those he himself called his 'Roman Catholic fellow-countrymen'. In 1908 he defended the Liberal government's decision to establish a university system in Ireland on the grounds that it was the state's duty to 'satisfy the aspirations of those for the remedy of whose grievances it is put forward'. He recognized that Trinity College, Dublin, was formally undenominational, but freely acknowledged that it had a Protestant atmosphere which Catholics could only find disagreeable. It was, he said, up to the new university institutions to prove their worth; and they could only do this if they avoided framing their curriculum on narrow sectarian differences, whether Roman Catholic or Presbyterian, and managed their business 'on the broad basis of liberty, which can alone gain success in education in any country'. He hoped one day to see them, and Trinity College, joining in 'one great national university'. Carson retained these convictions through thick and thin to the end of his political life. In February 1921 he advised the Ulster Unionist Council to 'see that the Catholic minority have nothing to fear from the Protestant majority. ... While maintaining intact our own religion let us give the same rights to the religion of our neighbours' (Stewart, *Carson*, p. 120).

This brings us to the other cause for which Carson did not fight: the partition of Ireland and the creation of a Unionist state in the north. Carson placed himself at the head of Ulster Unionist resistance to the third Home Rule Bill in 1912, believing that there lay the rock on which the whole cause of Irish Home Rule must founder. If Ulster succeeded, Home Rule was dead. But as we shall see time and circumstance were to undo his grand design and bring about not only partition but Home Rule in the north of Ireland – Ulster Unionist home rule – and leave Carson with the consequences of his failure: a six-county Northern Ireland state. When the Ulster Nationalist leader Joseph Devlin taunted him in 1920 with having got 'all he ever asked for, and more' in the Government of Ireland Act which established Northern Ireland, Carson retorted 'No, I have not! If I had got all that I ever asked for there would never have been a Home Rule Bill' (Colvin, *Carson*, iii, pp. 284-5).

Let us now consider the causes for which Carson did take off his coat: those of Ireland, of the United Kingdom, and the British Empire. Carson saw these as interdependent, as a set of overlapping circles, within each of which was to be found common ground, common links: break a circle, snap a link, and the whole must disintegrate.

In this belief Carson was not of course without intellectual ancestors: Edmund Burke had maintained in 1796 that 'Ireland cannot be separated one moment from England without losing every source of her present prosperity and even every hope for the future'; Burke, like Carson, supported Roman Catholic claims for the right to full and unadulterated citizenship of the Kingdom. W.E.H. Lecky, the great historian and political thinker of the late nineteenth century and, like Carson, a Trinity College man and a liberal in his early years, believed in a unitary British empire based upon mutual benefit. For the smaller units to benefit, the larger must have a steady political equilibrium, and liberty for the smaller units must be compatible with the stability of the whole.

But Lecky pointed out that Britain had its duties as well as its rights, and he bitterly opposed what he called the 'Jekyll and Hyde' attitude to the Union which he found prevalent in British political circles: the view that Ireland was regarded as 'an internal portion' of the United Kingdom 'when it was a question of taxation, and therefore entitled to no exemptions'; and a 'separate entity when it was a question of rating and therefore entitled to no relief'.

Lecky, like Carson, held that disloyalty in Ireland was subversive of civility and order, encouraging a disregard for the law which could only undermine and debase public life. As Crown prosecutor, Carson was in a position to remedy this: hence his unflinching and uncompromising attack on lawless elements in the Land League days. But while Carson was able to act, where Lecky could only exhort in print, in another respect he was less favourably positioned. In 1871 Lecky could still hope that the propertied classes might yet direct local political feeling, might yet recover the confidence of the people; Carson could harbour no such illusions. Landlordism by the turn of the century was a dead or dying social and political force, however much Irish landlords might yet hope to influence the policy of the British Unionist party over opposition to Home Rule. And whereas Lecky supported British Land Acts in the hope that they would create a conservative peasant propriety, Carson opposed them as yet another British assault on its only loyal people. Lecky may have been fighting a losing battle in the 1870s but by 1906 the battle was already lost and there could be no return to eighteenth-century patterns of social relations he hoped to see reconstructed in nineteenth-century Ireland.

Like Burke and Lecky, Carson was a Whig in politics, and since he lived in Ireland he was an Irish Whig, not only physically but also politically, in that he believed in the best possible government of Ireland, the maximum amount of liberty for its people, just and decent treatment for all irrespective of religion, and a progressive administration. In temperament, therefore, Carson was no Tory, nor reactionary, but Whiggism was a difficult style to practise in a democratic and populist political age. Carson was faced with war on two fronts: in Ireland a nationalist movement threatened plunder and disruption; but in Britain he confronted an equally dangerous enemy, political indifference, a lack of concern for Ireland, an inability of English politicians and public to understand the temperature and thought of the Irish people. Burke feared the development of a separating spirit in Ireland; Lecky feared its manifestation in England through ignorance and political blindness: Carson feared both.

Irish nationalism was Carson's obvious enemy, but he identified another, and in some respects more dangerous and insidious threat to the Union: the failure of British politicians and public to govern Ireland in a generous but firm spirit. Not for the sake of killing Home Rule with kindness, though Carson wanted to kill Home Rule; but more positively because Ireland, as an integral part of the United Kingdom, deserved no less than good and equal government. Carson did not subscribe to Conservative political expediency or, as it was called, 'Conservative Unionism', between 1887 and 1906. He held that it was in the Union parliament that Irish interests could best be defended; it was here that Irish political influence, and even power, would most effectively and beneficially be exercised. This, of course, threw a great responsibility upon Irish Unionists, British Unionists, and the British parliamentary system. In 1896 Carson defended the cause of Irish teachers who were found to have a deficit in their pension fund. Carson advocated settlement by a simple grant; Gerald Balfour, Chief Secretary for Ireland, preferred to meet the deficiency by an increase of contributions. When Balfour petulantly retorted that 'all the Irish members will invariably come down to the house and press for money when they think it can be squeezed out of the Treasury', Carson was on his feet, his Irish pride stung, rebuking him for his 'unworthy' remarks; but, equally significantly, he warned Balfour that such a tone in the British parliament did not improve the position of Unionists in Ireland, or make their task in the House of Commons easier.

This exchange tells us two things about Carson and his cause. On a personal level it reveals that he was never prepared to put party loyalty, or personal advancement, above the cause of Ireland: and this he maintained to the end, as his resignation from the British government in January 1918 in defence of Irish interests shows. On a political level it illustrates the enormity of his task. For Carson could hardly hope to convince most Irishmen that Union was best – a belief the majority did not hold in 1886, still did not hold in 1912, and most emphatically rejected in the 1918 general election which swept Sinn Féin to power – and so he must convince most *Englishmen* that they must stand fast for the Union;

and that *they* must respond to loyal Ireland by behaving like loyal England, by placing Irish interests before even the immediate interests in England. Carson's appearances in Ulster stick in the memory as a kind of royal progress; his speeches, a mixture of plain, even homely, phrases and strong melodrama, appealed to the temperament of his Ulster Protestant audience. He made many more Unionist speeches in Great Britain, though, than he ever did in Ireland, north or south, for Carson had to keep Britain up to the mark. Even Gladstone, who espoused the cause of Home Rule and fought a general election on its behalf in 1886, admitted that for an Englishman to place Ireland first and foremost was 'against nature'.

There was – at least on the surface – a vital difference between Gladstone's and Carson's task; for Carson could appeal to British imperial pride, to her Protestant sentiment, still a force to be reckoned with – it was after all Rudyard Kipling who spoke darkly of

> The hells declared
> For such as serve not Rome

– and above all to her rather self-conscious sense of fair play. Was it in the best British tradition to place the Protestant people of Ulster under the heel of Dublin? To establish this point Carson organized Ulster's Solemn League and Covenant: 'The stronger they were', he claimed, 'the more moderate they could afford to be' (Colvin, ii, p.148). Moreover, the British Conservative – or (as it called itself) Unionist Party – enthusiastically took up Carson's cause. As leader of its Irish Unionist group – some twenty strong – in 1910, and as a respected politician who had survived the disastrous electoral defeat of 1906 when Unionist Cabinet ministers lost their seats all over the country, Carson was a highly influential figure. Moreover the Unionist Party had its own quarrel with the Liberals and their Irish allies, with in what Lord Selbourne once called the 'Home-rule-pro-Boer-little England-Socialist party' – a fine string of insults, especially provoked by the Peoples' Budget of 1909 which the Unionist – dominated House of Lords rejected, only of find their own power of veto over Commons legislation removed in the 1911 Parliament Act. Carson seemed to possess yet another advantage in the British political scene. The Liberal Party only reluctantly took up the cause of Irish Home Rule in 1912, allegedly (in the Unionists' opinion) as a reward to Redmond for his support of the Peoples' Budget and the Parliament Act – that 'corrupt bargain' made more corrupt by the fact that two general elections in 1910 left the Liberal government heavily if not absolutely, dependent on the Irish Parliamentary Party's support. And if Carson placed himself at the head of Ulster Unionist resistance to the third Home Rule Bill, and if he succeeded in demonstrating that Ulster meant business, would the Nationalists for their part want Home Rule without the north?

But beneath this apparent strength, Carson's purpose was deeply flawed. The Unionist Party, it was true, could hardly abandon its cause without suffering a major split, as it had only recently undergone over Tariff Reform, since British Unionists were divided at least three ways about Ireland: some stood for the Union and nothing but the Union; others favoured a federal reorganization of the whole United Kingdom as a way of meeting the difficulty; still others, among them the party leader Andrew Bonar Law, would be satisfied if the position of Ulster were secured. The party therefore backed Carson in his mission to defeat Home Rule. It was aware of the fact that while loyal Ulster enjoyed much support amongst the British public, that same public might, as Law admitted privately, 'decide that Ulster must not be coerced; but I think they are so sick of the whole Irish question that they would vote in favour of trying an experiment so long as the Ulster difficulty was solved' (Boyce, pp. 92-3). Carson found himself having at least to contemplate the idea of some fair and reasonable settlement of the Irish difficulty that would save Ulster, but fatally compromise the link between his beloved Ireland, the United Kingdom and the British empire.

Carson's two other assumptions, about what his enemies would do, were proving equally fragile. The Liberal government, reluctant though it may have been, was still the heir to the Gladstonian tradition, even if it had lost its old fire and fervour; and anyway it felt that it could not retreat before its Unionist opponents without seriously damaging its own reputation and forfeiting its right to be regarded as a government. If the Home Rule issue was a party political game, it was not one that the Liberals could lightly lose. Moreover, the Irish Parliamentary Party, while maintaining all the time that Ireland was a seamless garment, knew full well that it would be difficult to refuse a genuine offer of a settlement based on some special treatment of

Ulster. By 1913 and 1914 British public opinion was convinced that some kind of settlement of the Ulster crisis was preferable to civil war. As yet, however, none of the parties could extricate themselves from the predicament without loss of face or, even worse, party unity. In the summer of 1914 a grim and depressed Carson began to resign himself to the probability of civil conflict: Home Rule was moving towards the statute book; and there was no sign that his enemies would concede the great game of the Union.

The European crisis and Britain's entry into the First World War postponed the crisis in Ireland; but it also presented Carson with a personal political dilemma. He was a sincere British patriot precisely because he was a sincere Irish patriot. With the empire's very existence at stake, when so much depended on Britain winning the war, he must weigh in the balance his great causes, his three great causes, and must exercise a judgment of Solomon. Between 1914 and 1918 Carson's Unionism was compromised again and again. First he felt himself obliged to place the Ulster Volunteer Force (Carson's Army, as it was nicknamed) at the disposal of the War Office, and yet suffer the enormity of Asquith's placing of the Home Rule Bill on the statute book. 'I think this is a very unfortunate procedure by the Government', he wrote, 'as it will necessarily bring us back to a state of party warfare of a particularly bitter character'; but more grievous to him than party warfare was the impact of this on Ireland, where 'disunion' would be increased, and where

the idea of co-operation between the Ulster Volunteers and the Nationalist Volunteers will be out of the question, and any chance of ultimate agreement, wholly or partially, which might develop out of working together for the common interest of the country will have entirely disappeared, and a feeling of bitterness will be engendered which will render the situation hopeless as far as unity is concerned.

Carson felt he must remain silent on the matter because of the 'importance of presenting a united front to foreign nations' (Carson to H.A. Gwynnes, 7 August 1914).

In 1916 Carson was again forced to set his Unionism against the needs of the British war effort, and strike another balance. This time he had to urge the Ulster Unionists to accept Lloyd George's post-Easter Rising offer of partition and make shift for themselves, because to do otherwise would, he believed, seriously imperil Britain just when she was hoping for America's entry into the war on the allied side. Even while he was addressing the Ulster Unionists on 6 June 1916 he was handed a telegram bearing the news that Lord Kitchener and his staff had been lost at sea: 'Gentlemen,' he said, 'every day we have heart-breakings over these matters and these things make us think and think seriously' (Colvin, iii, pp.164-70). In 1917 he could only acquiesce in the Irish Convention which the government set up to remove the Irish Question from the political stage, and allow Britain to get on with the war; in 1918 he even briefly espoused the idea of a federated United Kingdom – an idea which he had earlier rejected – because, he said, 'the Union, which I regard as the keystone of the British Commonwealth, may nevertheless be preserved upon the principles of a true federation'. Federalism combined equality 'between the nations which are to be the federal units' and the securing to the central parliament of an 'actual and active supremacy'. But by the end of the war, as member of parliament for the Duncairn constituency in Belfast, he was driven back into his Ulster corner, warning the government that if it tried to take away one jot or tittle of Ulster's rights he would 'call out the Ulster Volunteers' – a threat which provoked a storm of criticism in Great Britain, and an apology from a least one British Conservative who declared that he regretted ever having supported Carson in the pre-war Home Rule struggle. And all this – this decline and fall – took place despite Carson's attainment of high office in the war: Attorney General in 1915; First Lord of the Admiralty in 1917; membership of the War Cabinet in 1917-18. For not even Carson's political advancement could prevent the Irish Question becoming one of those old quarrels which the post-war Coalition government of Unionists and Liberals, led by Lloyd George, was elected to resolve; and resolve on a rational, non-partisan basis. Carson's illustrious moment on the stage of modern political history could not save the Union, the guiding star of his political life.

Carson's connection with the Irish Question in its last phase between 1919 and 1921 was a bitter and disappointed experience. He would not follow those southern Irish Unionists, led by Lord Midleton, who from 1918 sought an accommodation with nationalism; for Carson still held, as he had always held, that there was no place for his loyal men under their new political masters, whether Redmondite or Sinn Féin. He abstained from voting on the Government of Ireland Act, regarding it as a necessary protection for the loyal north, though he did not see why the Ulster Unionists should be obliged to accept a parliament in Belfast which they did not desire: 'we want to remain with you. Do not turn us out' (Colvin, iii, pp. 380-85). He acknowledged, however, that in this matter he would be guided by the wishes of the Ulster Unionists, who in the event negotiated a six- rather than nine-county parliament as a better alternative than Dublin rule, but his Irish Unionism could not be so easily reconciled to the Ireland of the coming times. Carson's magnificent yet wholly destructive speech on the Anglo-Irish Treaty in December 1921 warned the British of the consequences of their government's recently discovered policy of settlement in Ireland. As an Irish Unionist, Carson felt betrayed by Britain, but he also felt that Britain had betrayed herself. She had failed, in the end, to stand up for what she believed in, for British rule and British civilization, not only in Ireland but in the whole of the British empire:

If you tell your Empire in India, in Egypt and all over the world that you have not got the men, the money, the pluck, the inclination and the backing to restore order in a country within twenty miles of your own shore, you may as well begin to abandon the attempt to make British rule prevail throughout the Empire at all.(Cambell, *F.E. Smith*, p. 576)

Britain's reputation as a strong, firm but fair upholder of law and order, which Carson fought for in his own way in the law courts of Ireland during the Plan of Campaign – that of a 'justice-loving, religion-loving, and in every respect … trusted nation' – was now fatally undermined.

Sir Edward Carson had a political vision, we might conclude, but without the practical political means of attaining it. He had no strong political base in southern Ireland, so he depended upon his ability to sell his political views to other, more substantial, groups: to Ulster Unionists, and British Conservatives, The support of others however could only be conditional and provisional; in the end they had their own interest to consult. They can hardly be blamed for so doing Carson's own grand design was inextricably linked with the political interest from which *he* came, that of the Protestant of southern Ireland. When Irish Unionism failed, so did the vision that was based upon Britain's importance to Ireland,

Ireland's importance to Britain, and the importance of both to the British empire. And when that grand design collapsed, as it did in 1921, then Sir Edward Carson's personal and political cause was lost.

But what, if anything, did Ireland lose? Certainly, we might say, much that it could afford to lose: an ascendancy caste; the rule of a government and parliament that the majority of her people had rejected through the ballot box since the 1870s. Nevertheless, we must remind ourselves that Carson's Ireland was and – had he succeeded – would have been a united Ireland. A study of Carson the loser makes us think about the compatibility of Irish freedom and Irish unity, that great dilemma at the heart of our modern political history.

FURTHER READING

The standard work on Lord Carson is still I. Colvin and E. Marjoribanks, *The Life of Lord Carson* (3 vols, London 1932-6), partly because of its detail, and partly because much of the evidence used by the biographers was destroyed in the bombing during the Second World War. H. Montgomery Hyde's *Carson* (London 1953, reprinted 1979) uses some new material untouched by Colvin and Marjoribanks and is a satisfying one-volume life. A.T.Q. Stewart's *Edward Carson* (Dublin 1982) is a very useful brief account, but could have benefited from a consideration of Carson's place in British politics generally. It is well written. R.B. McDowell's 'Edward Carson' in C.C. O'Brien, *The Shaping of Modern Ireland* (London 1960), sought to rescue Carson, and Irish Unionism, from the view that both stood for a merely negative tradition in Irish history. On the content of Carson's intellectual and ideological development, and in particular on his relationship to Lecky, see Yvonne Dineen, 'The Problem of Stability in a Democratic Age: the Ideas of W.E.H. Lecky' (University of Wales Ph. D. 1986). The paradox of Carson's political career, and his connection with the Ulster Unionists, is beautifully delineated by J.C. Beckett in the 'Carson: Unionist and Rebel' in F.X. Martin (ed.), *Leaders and Men of the Easter Rising: Dublin, 1916* (London 1967), reprinted in J.C. Beckett, *Confrontations: Studies in Irish History* London 1972). Patrick Buckland, *Irish Unionism 1: The Anglo-Irish and the New Ireland, 1885-1922* (Dublin 1972), offers the fruits of massive research on the wider context of Irish Unionism in general. Carson's influence in British politics is surveyed generally in D.G. Boyce, 'British Conservative Opinion, the Ulster Question and the partition of Ireland 1912-1921' in *Irish Historical Studies*, XVII (1970), and at a crucial juncture in the late pages of John Cambell's biography, *F.E. Smith , Earl of Birkenhead* (London 1983).

IRISH
RELIEF FUND
BAZAAR
MADISON SQUARE GARDEN
FOR THE BENEFIT OF
THE FAMILIES OF IRISH MARTYRS AND PRISONERS
OCTOBER 14TH 22
1 PM TO 11 PM
GENERAL ADMISSION 50¢

The Execution of James Connolly

XIII

JAMES CONNOLLY (1868-1916)
and Irish Socialism

PAUL BEW

THE IRISH LABOUR LEADER, James Connolly, executed by the British following the 1916 Easter Rising, was exceptional among socialist theoreticians in being an unskilled labourer. He educated himself to a high level while coping with the demands of political activity, physical labour and a family. In Joseph Lee's view, his writings on modern Irish history, flung down at odd moments snatched from the daily grind of eking out a living, are, despite their many flaws, worth more than those of all his professional contemporaries combined. Connolly's life represents a triumph of human will and intelligence over adverse circumstances.

Connolly, born in Edinburgh in 1868, was a remarkably brave man who made a valuable contribution to the working-class movement in Belfast and in Dublin, and also in America, where he was involved in the first decade of this century in what proved to be the eventual high-water-mark of American socialism. The Irish-American working class held a pivotal place among the American proletariat for it was they, of all ethnic groups, who alone had representation in the older, skilled and relatively privileged trades, as well as in the unskilled labouring category. They were in a way the core of the American industrial working class, and in view of his own later development in Ireland it is interesting to note Connolly's rueful analysis that they had been put off socialism by the American left's commitment to anti-clerical, anti-religious propaganda.

As one of the men of 1916 who displayed an exemplary heroism both during the fighting and at the hour of his death, Connolly's name rapidly became enshrined within the pantheon of Ireland's republican heroes. Yet the distinctiveness of his contribution to the insurrection, the conditional nature of his decision to ally himself with the Irish Republican Brotherhood, and his critical attitude towards the aims and methods of Irish bourgeois nationalism, were quickly obscured in the truimphalist celebrations of an independent nation-state. In this way Connolly became a loser: not a defeated or forgotten man, but more ironically one who contributed so much to the success of a movement to which he was ultimately and fundamentally opposed.

In recent years, however, Connolly may be said to have re-emerged from the clouds of nationalist obfuscation. The Northern 'troubles' have stimulated interest in his legacy to an unusual degree. Already the subject of a major if uncritical biography published by Desmond Greaves in 1961, Connolly had no fewer than six-book-length studies devoted to him between 1971 and 1981 (see Further Reading). And as late as 1988 Austen Morgan's biography has argued prevocatively that Connolly's drift towards revolutionary nationalism was no mere error, reversal or degeneration, but a clear-headed calculation based upon his recognition of the collapse of international socialism amidst the crisis of the First World War. Connolly's recent record thus compares well with that of the other great leader of 1916, Pearse, who, despite his relatively cautious social views and his conventional religiosity, which make him a more typical exemplar of Irish nationalism, had been the subject of only one major biography in this period. Meanwhile, though we are still without a complete scholarly edition of Connolly's works, numerous editions of his texts have been issued, and many pamphlets, articles and sections in books have been devoted to him.

Yet Connolly remains a strangely ambiguous and divided figure, claimed as an inspiration to many movements and opinions deeply opposed to one another. Why do we remain so troubled about him? There is little doubt that the Northern crisis helps greatly to explain this phenomenon, providing yet another rehearsal of that peculiar concatenation of nationalism, Catholicism and socialism which have been such a feature of modern Irish history and of Connolly's career in particular.

What are the relationships which exist, or may be said to exist, between Catholicism, nationalism and socialism? What is the 'correct' attitude towards the Protestant working class in the North which is stubbornly resistant to Catholic nationalism, though happy to accept the benefits of the British Labour movement's great achievement, the Welfare State. There are other interesting debates concerning Connolly's view of the role of the socialist party and trade union activity, but it is the Northern conflict and the issues about socialism and nationalism it had raised that have again pushed Connolly to the forefront.

Following his return from America in 1908, Connolly was absorbed in evaluating the significance of the Ulster question in the years 1910 to 1914, when his work as a labour organizer in Belfast brought him face to face with the sectarianism of that city. Connolly's analysis of the 'northern question', has been subjected to much criticism. It has been argued, for example, that when Connolly claimed during his controversy with the pro-Union socialist William Walker that 'only the force of religious bigotry remains an asset to Unionism', he seriously underestimated the economic and social basis for the Unionist mobilization like any conventional, middle-class nationalist of his day. At the very least it was a remarkable flight of fancy which allowed Connolly to claim – in the face of bitter claims to the contrary from both the Unionists bourgeois and the working class – that 'there is no economic class in Ireland today whose interest as a class is bound up with the Union'. Because he felt so much that bourgeois Irish nationalism was a sham, Connolly found it difficult to take Ulster Unionism seriously. In his introduction to *The Worker's Republic* (Dublin 1951) William McMullen recalled such a moment:

[Connolly] found the Northern environment trying and uncongenial and it was only with difficulty he could be patient with the odd stolid Orangeman whom he encountered in his propaganda work up to this. One such occasion was when he was speaking at Library Street on a Sunday evening and was expatiating on Irish history when one of this type interrupted him, and drawing a copy of he Solemn League and Convenant from his pocket brandished it in the air and remarked there would be no Home Rule for Ireland and he and his thousands of co-signatories would see to it. Connolly, with a sardonic smile, advised him to take the document home and frame it, adding 'your children will laugh at you'.

In Connolly's view the shared experience of exploitation would eventually overcome the artificial divisions within the Belfast working class. He wrote:

Despite their diverse origin, the workers of Ireland are bearers of a common spoliation and sufferers from a common bondage ... the rallying cries of the various parties led by the various factions of our masters, are but sound and fury, signifying nothing to us in our present needs and struggles ...

But the Orangeman's children probably did not, as Connolly had expected, laugh at him; and today if his grandchildren have moved away from Orangeism it is much more likely to be due to the seduction of upward mobility than the pressures of class solidarity.

Yet despite these serious problems there are still those, who perhaps a little piously, take a more sympathetic view of Connolly's role in Belfast, arguing that even if he had understood more fully the complexities of Unionism there was little he could have done about it, and that, at the least, his prediction that partition would usher in a 'carnival of reaction' on both sides of the border has some merit to it.

Even if we accept the burden of recent critiques of Connolly's views on the North, it is worth pointing out that he never accepted the glib assumption that sectarianism on the nationalist side was not a serious problem. Instead, he bitterly denounced the Ancient Order of Hibernians, the powerful and widely popular Catholic – only body which wielded much influence at the heart of Home Rule nationalism even though a Parnell or a Wolfe Tone could not have formed it. In Connolly's words it was this body and not the Orange Order which was the 'greatest curse yet introduced into the political and social life of Ireland'.

Too much concern with his attitude to the North has obscured our understanding of Connolly in his own context. As a result one important question is rarely asked? What was Connolly's relationship to the mainstream nationalist movement in the Ireland of his day? In his *The Modernization of Irish Society*, published in 1973, Joseph Lee raised a point which fourteen years later has yet to be adequately addressed:

Connolly's fatal tactical error [Lee argued] was his reluctance to acknowledge the existence of rural Ireland. His Edinburgh life had made him a 'townie' to the core. The programme of his socialist party in 1896 contains almost nothing on agriculture. His solitary excursion to south-east Ireland brought clear insight into the economic problems of small farms but no understanding of peasant psychology. (p.151)

As Connolly once blithely understated it himself, 'Peasant proprietary is somewhat of a hindrance to the spread of socialist ideas.' There is nothing in Connolly's work to compare remotely with the efforts devoted by Lenin or Kautsky to the analysis of tendencies of development within Russian and German agriculture, or indeed the political debates linked to the land issue.

The Home Rule party of Connolly's day was committed to 'Ireland for the Irish' and the 'land for the people', but what did these phrases mean? The Irish nationalist party of the 1890s and 1900s was, in theory, committed to the breaking up of large grazing farms and their redistribution among the poor and landless. As the historian Sean Connolly pointed out in 1987, some have been tempted to see in this conflict between highly capitalized ranchers and a land-hungry rural poor the true location for Ireland's potential social revolution. In reality nationalist leadership was forced to recognize that the cattle trade was crucial to the livelihood of the great majority of Irish farmers; so it is hardly surprising that many of the ranch leaders were themselves shown to have grazing interests.

Now it seems clear from Connolly's cynical comments on the issue in his *Worker's Republic* journal that he was fully aware of the flawed, ambiguous nature of Irish rural class conflict. He linked this with the way in which the Home Rule party, which would happily talk about expropriation of the landlord's interest, would prove itself to be highly sensitive to property rights in an urban and capitalist setting. Nevertheless, Roy Foster is almost certainly right to argue in his *Modern Ireland 1600-1972* that Connolly ought to have devoted more thought to the implications of rural embourgeoisment.

In his *Labour in Irish History*, published in 1910, Connolly contended that the Land League and subsequent land legislation had developed the epoch of capitalist farming in Ireland. But this had happened at precisely the moment when agriculture was becoming an international industry – with a 50 per cent increase in the area under cultivation in the the years between 1840 and 1870. The Irish farmer thus found himself in competition with the large-scale, more mechanized farming of North America. In Connolly's view, expressed as early as 1898, only social ownership of all the resources of Ireland and a protected economy could save the rural population from impoverishment: 'We are left no choice but socialism or universal bankruptcy.'

This hardly avoids this problem. It is a retreat into an abstract 'purist' solution which had bedevilled Irish socialism throughout the twentieth century, ignoring, as Marx did earlier and with rather more excuse, the social and political weight of the Irish rural bourgeoisie. In this regard, it is worth looking at Connolly's article in *The Harp* for August 1908 entitled 'Michael Davitt: A text for a revolutionary lecture'. Here, Connolly attempted to come to terms with the meaning of the Land League crisis of 1879 to 1882: 'We believe', he writes, 'that a close study of the events of that time would immensely benefit the militant socialists of all countries'. Connolly's view of the Land League was positive: its leaders had transformed Irish nationalism from a 'sterile parliamentarism' into a a 'virile force ... The Land League made adhesion to the cause of the tenants synonymous with the call of Irish patriotism, and thus emphasized the point we have so often laboured, *viz.* – that the Irish question is a social question.'

Yet, as Connolly admitted, the 'Land League did not entirely succeed in its mission'. Failure lay amongst its leadership: 'the promoters were not in agreement as to their ultimate ideal and were unable to educate their followers against the fallacy of accepting concessions which divided and disorganized their forces when at the flood tide of success.'

Such an interpretation places too much emphasis on the leadership and too little on the nature of the Land League as a mass movement. More revealingly, describing the working of his movement, Connolly lays exclusive stress on the tactics which expressed the communal solidarity of the poor peasantry, ignoring equally significant tactics which pointed up class division within the Irish peasantry as stronger farmers imposed their price for participation in the struggle against the landlords. In short, by 1881 a substantial rural bourgeoisie had shown its hand and was prepared to accept limits to the pace of agrarian change as protection against challenge from below.

Nationalist leadership in the succeeding generation was therefore always caught uneasily between pressure from the rural 'haves' and the rural 'have nots'. By 1914 roughly two-thirds of the Irish peasantry had got what they wanted – their land. They no longer needed a party at Westminster to wring further reforms; indeed, they were sometimes irritated by the Irish Party's concessions to the rural poor. Also, the Westminster parliament was beginning to talk worryingly about land taxes, etc., to finance social reform. The bottom one-third of discontented Irish farmers resented the old Irish Parliamentary Party's failure to do anything much for them. In the emotional circumstances created by the Easter rising both sections of the Irish farming community found they had no material reason not to ditch the Irish party and embrace Sinn Fein; indeed the balance of material reason (as well as the ideological) favoured such a ditching. In some places, the land-hungry men gave Sinn Féin its radical tinge; more often the satisfied conservative majority imposed its vision on the new movement, and later on the new Irish parliament.

The clue, then, to understanding Connolly is to realize that, as Henry Patterson has argued, he slid from the view that the 'working class could play a leading role in the national revolution to the very different one that there could be no national revolution without the leadership of the working class'. In a 1987 article, Bob Purdie has argued shrewdly that Connolly's great work, *Labour in Irish History*, 'sheds no light on his joining the 1916 rebellion and certainly does not offer a justification of it', and instead emphasizes the importance of class and a critical disdain for the conventional nationalism of Connolly's day. Against this, Connolly would undoubtedly reply that he had demonstrated that the Irish national revolution could only be properly conducted as a socialist revolution. This in its way is a dramatic thesis which certainly exploits the ambiguity not the term 'Irish freedom'; yet it works largely by ignoring in a solipsistic fashion those powerful social forces which strongly supported a more conservative conception of national independence and which, to this day, have prevented a Connolly-style marriage of nationalism and socialism in Ireland.

There are differing views of Connolly's evolution. For Owen Dudley Edwards and Bernard Ranson, writing in 1973, Connolly's movement from conventional socialism to revolutionary nationalism marks him out as 'probably the most significant contributor to left-wing political theory to have emerged in the last hundred years'. Geoff Eley, on the other hand, wrote in 1981: 'It is difficult to regard Connolly's movement from the principled affirmation of an independent socialist politics in the Irish Socialist Republican Party (1896-1903) and the Socialist Party of Ireland (from 1910) to the uncritical Irish nationalism of 1916 as anything but a degeneration.' And in Eley's view it is the later positions of Connolly which have regrettably endured: the strategic identity of nationalist and socialists goals, the dogmatic belief that the working class would play the leading role in any successful national revolution, and the concomitant disregard for both the peasantry and the Protestant working class.

Brendan Clifford (1986) has been even more critical:

For many years [Connolly] persuaded himself that the prospects for socialism were better in an independent Ireland then in Britain. But the Home Rule Bill concentrated his mind wonderfully on social reality in the south of Ireland. He said there would probably not be a single socialist member of the Irish parliament. But this did not shake his nationalism. He continued to demand independence even while saying that the Irish Parliament would be the most reactionary in Europe. But he began to plead with the British Labour Party to demand the same Labour measures be written into the Home Rule Bill – as Britain's parting imperialist gift to Ireland.

There are still many today looking for similarly benign parting imperialist gifts in order to keep the working class of the North (Catholic or Protestant) in the style to which it has become accustomed Others accept that here are indeed difficulties and contradiction in Connolly's thought, but argue that he was still correct to intervene in the Easter Rising of 1916 to imprint the priorities of radical republicanism (not socialism) on the nationalist project. Too much time, it is said, can be spent in the armchair pondering theoretical difficulties. The same admirers will argue that Connolly's predicted 'carnival of reaction' on both sides of the border following partition was largely justified by the development of both states. Neither Irish state was a model of liberal democracy in the 'twenties and 'thirties; in the North the influences of sectarianism and rigid conservatism were very strong; in the south, these same influences were compounded by the presence for a brief period (1933-4) of a mass fascist-style movement. In this sense, the 'carnival of reaction' prediction was justified. But what of the connection between Connolly's own actions in 1916 and the eventual outcome? There can be no doubt that the limited possibilities of conciliation in Ireland in the relatively peaceful period from 1890-1910 deteriorated rapidly when force or the threat of force became a serious factor in Irish political life. The sheer harshness of the 'settlements' north and south is indisputably related to the role of the gun in Irish politics; in this sense Connolly's 'carnival of reaction' was a self-fulfilling prophecy. This is the dark side of Connolly's legacy, a dark side all the more tragic given his undeniable greatness of character.

FURTHER READING

Owen Dudley Edwards and Bernard Ransom (eds), *James Connolly: Selected Political Writings* (London 1973), and P. Beresford Ellis, *James Connolly: Selected Writings* (Penguin 1971), are useful anthologies of Connolly's work. Austen Morgan, *James Connolly: A Political Biography* (Manchester 1988), is a revisionist *tour de force*, but even Morgan would admit that the late Desmond Greaves provided much important material on Connolly in his *The Life and Times of James Connolly* (London 1961). Greaves and Morgan are the two pillars of Connolly historiography, but there are many other individual contributions to the study of Connolly's life and thought. Notable special studies are Carl Reeve and Anne Barton Reeve, *James Connolly and the United States: The Road to the 1916 Rebellion* (New Jersey 1978); Manus O'Riordan, *Connolly in America* (Belfast 1980); Owen Dudley Edwards, *The Mind of an Activist James Connolly* (Dublin 1971); Bernard Ransom, *Connolly's Marxism* (London 1980); Roger Faligot, *Connolly et le Mouvement Revolutionnaire Irlandais* (Paris 1978). David Howell's treatment of Connolly in *A Lost Left* (London 1987) and Henry Patterson's in *Class Conflict and Sectarianism* (Belfast 1980) are exceptionally judicious. Connolly's views on the North of Ireland are discussed in Paul Bew, Peter Gibbon and Henry Patterson, *The State in Northern Ireland* (Manchester 1979), and in Paul Bew, 'Britain's Modern Irish Question', *Economy and Society* 10 (1981). His outlook on rural society is considered in Bew, *Conflict and Conciliation in Ireland* (Oxford 1987), and late nineteenth-century rural realities in Bew, *Land and the National Question* (Dublin 1978). Critical assessments of Connolly's alliance with nationalism can be found in Geoff Eley, 'The Left, the Nationalists and the Protestants', *Michigan*

Quarterly Review 22 (1981), and Brendan Clifford, 'The Belfast Dock Strike of 1907', *Belfast Magazine* 1 (1986). Many believe that Desmond Ryan's *James Connolly: His Life, Work and Writings* (Dublin 1924), the first book on Connolly, remains the best.

NOTES ON CONTRIBUTORS

PAUL BEW is Reader in Political Science at The Queen's University, Belfast. Among his recent publications are *Land and the National Question in Ireland* (Dublin 1978) and *Conflict and Conciliation in Irish Nationalism* (Oxford 1987).

D. G. BOYCE is Reader in Political Theory and Government at University College, Swansea. He is author of *Nationalism in Ireland* (London 1982) and editor of *The Revolution in Ireland 1879-1923* (London 1988).

CIARAN BRADY is Lecturer in Modern History at Trinity College, Dublin. He is editor (with Raymond Gillespie) of *Natives and Newcomers: Essays on the Making of Irish Colonial Society, 1534-1641* (Dublin 1986) and (with Mary O'Dowd and Brian Walker) of *An Illustrated History of Ulster* (London 1989).

LIAM BREATNACH is Lecturer in Irish at Trinity College, Dublin. He is author of *Uraicecht na Ríar: The Poetic Grades in Early Irish Law* (Dublin 1987) and editor (with Donnchadh Ó Corráin and K. R. McCone) of *Sages, Saints and Story-Tellers: Celtic Studies in Honour of Professor James Carney* (Maynooth 1989).

AIDAN CLARKE is Professor of Modern History at Trinity College, Dublin. He is author of *The Old English in Ireland, 1625-1641* (London 1966) and a contributor to *A New History of Ireland: Early Modern Ireland, 1534-1691* (Oxford 1976).

MARY E. DALY is Statutory Lecturer in Modern Irish History at University College, Dublin. Her publications include *Dublin: The Deposed Capital, 1860-1914* (Cork 1984) and *The Famine in Ireland* (Dublin 1986).

DAVID DICKSON is Senior Lecturer in Modern History at Trinity College, Dublin. He is author of *New Foundations: Ireland, 1660-1800* (Dublin 1987) and editor of *The Gorgeous Mask: Dublin, 1700-1850* (Dublin 1987).

PATRICK KELLY is Senior Lecturer in Modern History at Trinity College, Dublin. His critical edition of the writings of John Locke, *Locke on Money*, is to be published in two volumes by Oxford University Press in 1990.

MICHAEL LAFFAN is Lecturer in Modern Irish History at University College, Dublin. He is author of *The Partition of Ireland, 1911-1923* (Dublin 1983) and editor of *The Burden of German History, 1919-1945* (London 1987).

JAMES LYDON is Professor of Medieval History at Trinity College, Dublin. Among his publications are *The Lordship of Ireland in the Middle Ages* (Dublin 1972) and *Ireland in the Later Middle Ages* (Dublin 1973).

W. J. MC CORMACK is a free-lance writer. Among his publications are *Sheridan Le Fanu and Victorian Ireland* (Oxford 1980), *Ascendancy and Tradition in Anglo-Irish literary history from 1789 to 1939* (Oxford 1985) and *The Battle of the Books: Two Decades of Irish Cultural Debate* (Mullingar 1988).

JAMES MCGUIRE is Lecturer in Modern Irish History at University College, Dublin. He is editor (with Art Cosgrove) of *Parliament and Community: Historical Studies XIV* (Belfast 1983) and is joint editor of the journal *Irish Historical Studies*.

DONNCHADH Ó CORRÁIN is Associate Professor of Irish History at University College, Cork. He is author of *Ireland before the Normans* (Dublin 1972) and editor of *Peritia: A Journal of Medieval Studies*.